The One Year
Designer Genes Devo

Tyndale House Publishers, Inc.
Carol Stream, Illinois

The One Year®
Designer Genes
Devo

Ann-Margret Hovsepian

Visit Tyndale's exciting Web site at www.tyndale.com

TYNDALE and Tyndale's quill logo are registered trademarks of Tyndale House Publishers, Inc.

The One Year is a registered trademark of Tyndale House Publishers, Inc.

The One Year Designer Genes Devo

Designed by Jacqueline L. Nuñez
Edited by Stephanie Voiland

Published in association with the literary agency of Sanford Communications, 16778 SE Cohiba Ct., Damascus, OR 97015.

Library of Congress Cataloging-in-Publication Data
Hovsepian, Ann-Margret.
  The one year designer genes devo/Ann-Margret Hovsepian.
    p. cm.
  Includes index.
  ISBN-13: 978-1-4143-1359-7 (sc)
  ISBN 10: 1-4143-1359-4 (sc)
  1. Girls—Religious life—Juvenile literature. 2. Girls—Conduct of life—Juvenile literature. I. Title.
  BV4551.3.H68 2007
  248.8'2—dc22   2007012891

Printed in the United States of America
13 12 11 10 09 08 07
 7 6 5 4 3 2 1

Dedication

To my readers—
you are precious!
Girls like you have
a special place in my heart,
so you were my inspiration
in writing this book!

Special thanks . . .

To God, for my "designer genes"!

To my dear parents, for leading me to Christ, for long ago recognizing my talents and helping me
find the path that led me here, and for your unwavering love and support.

To my precious nieces, Alexis and Melissa, and nephew, Joshua,
for providing lots of "tween" inspiration over the last few years.

To their mom and my big sister, Ruth, for putting up with me during my tween years!

To Jonathan, for believing in this book from day one and urging me to write it,
and for your encouragement throughout the process.

To my editors at Tyndale, for your enthusiasm about this book and your wonderful help in putting it together.

To my agent, David Sanford, for making it all happen!

Contents

The Beginning of a Great Adventure

You're not a teenager yet. You're also not a kid anymore. You're smart, you can handle responsibilities, and you're starting to think for yourself . . . but you still want to have fun and be silly with your friends sometimes, right? These years of your life (between being a child and being a teenager) can be some of the best years of a girl's life. Some of my own best memories are from when I was nine to twelve years old. It's a time when you're discovering the world . . . and the world is discovering you!

So why does life as a girl seem so confusing at times? Why is it so hard to figure out stuff like friendships, family relationships, school, clothes, the future . . . even sex? Why do so many of us end up imitating not-so-great role models, thinking that if we talk or act or dress a certain way, we'll be grown up and more popular? The truth is, trying to fit into someone else's image usually ends up making us more confused about life.

In *Designer Genes*, we're going to try to answer some of these questions together. You'll discover how each of us was created in God's image. You were uniquely designed by Him, and He's got an awesome plan for your life! When God made you, He gave you a one-of-a-kind set of genes. Each of the billions of cells in your body contains about 30,000 of these tiny genes, and each one of them carries special instructions. Your God-given genes determine what color eyes you have, how tall you are, what your smile looks like, and all kinds of other characteristics that make you uniquely you!

Isn't it exciting to realize how much love and care God put into designing you? Wearing designer jeans may get you a bit of attention for a short time by a few people . . . but I hope that, through *Designer Genes*, you will learn that it's not what you look like on the outside that matters. It's your God-given designer genes that make you the wonderful person you are!

Are you ready to get to know your Designer?

Let the Experiment Begin!

For the next 365 days, *Designer Genes* will take you through all the exciting, terrifying, fun, challenging, and crazy experiences that make these years so unforgettable! The cool thing about this experiment is that you don't need any complicated equipment or any scientific knowledge. Get yourself a Bible (if you don't have one, you or your parents can probably get one from a nearby church or bookstore), a nice pen, and if you'd like, a blank notebook or journal. Some devos suggest extra activities that just won't fit on the page, so a notebook will be perfect for those times.

Every week we'll look at a different topic that you're either dealing with now or will soon. These fifty-two topics have been divided into seven main sections: Your Body, Your Relationships, Growing Up, Your Soul, The Things You Do, The World around You, and The Media and You.

You'll see that each week's section is just a few pages long. Easy peasy! There's a short Bible reading for each day of the week, along with a question to answer or a sentence to complete in the space provided. For each devo, there are also puzzles, interesting facts, creative activities, challenges, and lots more!

When you finish reading *Designer Genes*, I hope you'll let me know how you liked it, how it helped you, and what else you'd like to talk about!

Okay, if you're ready for the excitement to begin, turn the page!

Section 1
YOUR BODY

From appetite to genes to zits,
your Designer can tell you everything
you need to know about your physical
development, health, and beauty. (He
has even provided an
instruction manual!)

The Skin You're In

Are You a Body or a Soul?

"The body is just a shell for the real person."
Author unknown

Here's something to think about: _____ [fill in your name]
is the girl who lives *inside* your body. . . . Your body is just the
container for your soul! (*Soul* might not be a word you use or hear
much, but it just describes the spiritual part of you, which is different from the physical part of you.) Your body will get older and die
one day, but your soul will live forever. Although you should take
care of your body, the really beautiful part of you is who you are
on the inside.

Real vs. Ideal

Studies show that in the last fifty years, the young women who
appear in magazines or compete in beauty pageants have become thinner and thinner . . . while the average woman is getting
heavier. Models used to weigh only 8 percent less than the average
woman, but today they weigh 23 percent less! That means that
there is a much bigger difference these days between "real" girls
and the "ideal" ones we see on TV and in magazines—the ones we
think we're supposed to look like!

No wonder so many of us girls are unhappy about our body
image. We feel a lot of pressure to change our appearance. Here
are several ways some of us try to look perfect.

(Of course, these things in themselves aren't necessarily wrong, but they can be if they start controlling our thoughts and our lives.)

 Going on diets

 Using makeup

 Whitening teeth

 Having cosmetic surgeries, such as fixing your nose, pushing back your ears, or getting breast implants

 Dyeing hair

 Straightening hair

 Shaving, waxing, plucking

What are some other ways?

If you're not happy with your looks, you're not alone! But did you know that, no matter how you feel, you are already beautiful? Beauty is not about looking like a supermodel. Becoming beautiful is about discovering—and appreciating—the natural beauty that God has already given you and letting it shine through, from the inside out!

Beauty Tips

"When I was a child, my mother [said] that to put a beautiful dress and perfume on a dirty body was like putting icing on gingerbread. No matter how sweet the topping, the taste of the ginger would cut through."
Michelle McKinney Hammond, author of *The Diva Principle*

There's nothing wrong with wanting to look nice, as long as we don't make that our main priority. (Spending too much time obsessing about hair or clothes can keep us from developing our relationships with God and others, as well as other important interests.)

To look your best, start off with a clean body, washed hair, brushed teeth, and neatly trimmed nails. Drinking lots of water, being active, and getting enough sleep will also make you look healthy, which is always attractive. Finally, nothing beats a real, heartfelt smile!

God loves beauty—that's not hard to figure out when we look at how He created this earth and everything in it. So it's natural for us to enjoy looking at beautiful things . . . and to want to look beautiful too! The problem is that sometimes we get confused about what true beauty is. We may think it's about having perfectly white teeth or shiny, long hair. The truth is, different people find different things beautiful! Let's remember that letting God change our hearts and characters (our designer genes) to be more like His will make us beautiful in the ways that really matter.

January 1—Genesis 1:26-31

These verses say that you were made in God's image! How does that help you with the way you feel about yourself?

January 2—1 Samuel 16:7

My thoughts about judging or being judged based on appearance:

January 3—Proverbs 31:30

Dear God, please teach me that beauty . . .

January 4—Isaiah 53:2-5

These verses predicted what Jesus would be like and what would happen to Him about 900 years before He was born. How does this passage speak to you about the importance we give to outward appearance?

January 5—1 Peter 3:3-6

I'm not married, but these verses still teach me that . . .

January 6—Matthew 23:25-28

What do these verses say about appearing beautiful only on the outside?

January 7—1 Corinthians 3:16-17

My thoughts about how I should treat my body:

Be Smart!

Tip #1: Remember that the beautiful girls you see in magazines and on the screen look the way they do thanks to special lighting, lots of makeup, airbrushing, and digital touch-ups to get rid of pimples, wrinkles, crooked teeth, and other imperfections. If *they* don't look perfect in real life, why should you?

Tip #2: It might help to know that guys feel just as insecure about their looks as you do . . . so just try to be yourself around them! If it doesn't seem like you're concerned about looking perfect, they won't feel like they need to look perfect either.

Is Fashion Your Passion?

Take a "Clothes"-er Look

Have you noticed that a lot of girls in our society are obsessed with clothes and fashion? No matter how many shoes or bags or tops they have, they would always be happy to have more! What about you? Do you put too much importance on what's in your closet . . . or do you appreciate what you have and try to help others who have less?

Here's a little self-test. Grab a pencil and take a little walk around your room. Count how many of these things you have. How many of those items did you wear at least twenty times in the past year? Write that number in the last column.

Item	I have . . .	I've worn . . .
Footwear (shoes, boots, sandals)		
Shirts (T-shirts, long-sleeved shirts, tanks)		
Pants (jeans, capris, shorts)		
Skirts and dresses		
Sweaters and sweatshirts		
Jackets and coats		
Socks		
Belts, scarves, and hats		
Purses		
Jewelry (count a pair of earrings just once)		

Surprised by how much you have? Disappointed? No matter what numbers you wrote down, you can be pretty sure that there are girls around the world who have much less . . . and some who may not even have everything on the list. They may have one pair of shoes and a couple of outfits to wear all year long. They can't go shopping and pick out things they like. They wear what they have.

Here's something else to think about: A lot of the clothes we wear are made by very poor people in other parts of the world. The clothes *they* wear are often the old, worn out, or out-of-style clothes that we got tired of and gave away. Does that seem fair?

Ask God to help you have a proper attitude about clothes . . . and to give you a heart that thinks of other people's *needs* before your *wants*.

Don't Be a Fashion Slave!

"Fashion is an imposition, a rein on freedom."
Golda Meir, first female prime minister of Israel

In simple language, Mrs. Meir was saying that designers and trends put pressure on us to dress a certain way, taking away our freedom to decide what colors and styles we like.

If you dress just like most other girls, what's so special about your style? Why let fashion designers—people who don't even know you—tell you what to wear? It's normal to want to fit in with your friends, but don't buy clothes you're not comfortable with just because someone else tells you they're "in." Instead, when you go clothes shopping, look for things that suit your style and make you feel confident. Remember to make sure they also please God! (We'll talk about this some more next week.)

The Changing Room

As you do this week's devotions, ask yourself these questions: How often do I go to the mall? How often do I buy things I don't need? How much of my money do I spend on clothes? How often do I obsess over what to wear? How often do I give my money to people in need?

At the end of the week, write down some ways you could change the way you shop.

It's normal to want to fit in with the rest of the girls at school or in your neighborhood, and there's nothing wrong with looking stylish. But the Bible teaches us not to fit into the mold or pattern of the world. Going along with the crowd can get you into sticky situations! For example, wearing jeans that sit too low on your hips or tops that hug you too tightly can attract embarrassing or awkward attention from guys. Be careful about spending too much time following trends. God can give you the wisdom you need to make good decisions about what you buy. Remember: You may not wear designer *jeans* . . . but you have been created with designer *genes!*

January 8—Romans 12:1-2
Who or what do your thoughts and desires tend to follow? Who or what *should* they follow?

January 9—Luke 12:27-28
I shouldn't worry about the clothes I wear because . . .

January 10—James 2:1-4
What does the Bible say about judging people by how well they are dressed?

January 11—Ezekiel 11:11-12

What can you learn from this verse about behaving or dressing like the people who don't believe in God?

January 12—Proverbs 23:23

What should you want more than the things you'd like to buy?

January 13—2 Corinthians 3:18

Instead of following the trends of the world, I should become more like . . .

January 14—Luke 12:31

You will have everything that you need in life if you do what?

Smart Shopping

When you see something you want to buy (whether it's clothes, accessories, music, or even gadgets), ask yourself: *Do I really love it?* Don't waste your money on something you're only going to like for a day and then get bored of.

If you really want to shop wisely, first ask yourself if you *need* it. You may have enough money to buy what you want, but will you be pleasing God? Is there something else He would want you to spend your money on?

Remember: Trends come and go quickly. That bright green and orange beaded bag may look cool now, but if that style goes out in a few months, you'll wish you had saved your money for something else . . . or used it to help someone else!

Be Aware of What You Wear!

What Are You Trying to Say?

Did you know your clothes can talk? Jewelry and T-shirts often have symbols or images on them—and these can be positive or negative. Be aware of what you buy, because as a Christian, you don't want people to think you agree with beliefs or ideas that go against what God teaches. Here are some examples of symbols you should know about:

Zodiac signs: The symbols you find on horoscopes come from astrology, and the Bible warns us not to get involved with that (see Deuteronomy 18:10-12). (We'll talk more about this in July—"Dangerous Stuff.") God wants us to trust Him with our futures, not some made-up ideas about how the stars and planets are lined up.

Anarchism: People who use this symbol don't respect authority (such as parents, the government, or teachers). For more on why God tells us to honor our leaders, see 1 Peter 2:13-14 and Ephesians 6:1-2.

Yin and yang: This symbol comes from the Tao religion, which teaches that an equal amount of evil and good exists in the world. The Bible teaches that God has power over everything in the world, including the devil. God's goodness will overcome every evil enemy. (See 1 John 4:4; 5:4; and Revelation 17:14.)

Skull and crossbones: A lot of clothes and accessories for young people have "cute" images of a skull and crossbones, or just a skull. But for many years, the skull has been a symbol of death, danger, poison, violence, fear, rebellion, and even some types of magic.

Ankh: This ancient Egyptian symbol may look like a cross, but it is actually the hieroglyph standing for fertility and sex.

Show Some Respect!

Dressing modestly and appropriately doesn't only show respect to the people around you. It also shows that you respect yourself! Just because "everyone" does something, it doesn't mean it's right or good or smart. Modesty doesn't mean you have go around in grandma clothes. You *can* look cute without causing people to look at you in a way that makes you uncomfortable. You *can* wear nice clothes without causing guys to stumble. And you *can* be stylish without displeasing God or sacrificing your self-respect.

KEEP THESE TIPS IN MIND:

 In hot weather, tiny tops and short shorts are *not* the best things to wear! Besides showing off too much of your body, they don't protect your skin from the sun. In many hot countries around the world, people wear clothes that cover up their arms and legs but are made of light fabrics.

You don't need body piercings, tattoos, dyed hair, or heavy makeup to fit in. Looking as natural as you can is much more attractive.

At church, make sure your clothes are respectful and decent. Remember that you, and others, are there to worship God. You don't want to be distracted by your clothes, and you don't want other people to be either.

Your clothes and jewelry shouldn't make it look like you're screaming for attention. If you're dressed nicely but modestly, people will notice *you*—your personality, talents, and who you are on the inside—not just your outfit. If your outfit attracts too much attention, that's what people will focus on. And that's not what you want. As a girl who belongs to God, you should try to show God's character in your life . . . even in the way you dress.

January 15—1 Timothy 2:9-10
What should people see when they look at you?

January 16—Romans 13:14
Who or what should you "put on" every morning? How can you do that?

January 17—Colossians 3:12-14
What kind of spiritual "clothes" should you wear?

January 18—1 Peter 5:5
Why does the Bible teach us to be humble?

January 19—Isaiah 61:10
I can feel joy like Isaiah did because . . .

January 20—Romans 6:13
What does this verse teach you about how you present your body by the way you dress?

January 21—Revelation 22:14-15
What "robes" do you think this verse is talking about? How can you wash your robes?

Mirror, Mirror, on the Wall . . .
The best time to make sure your clothes are modest is before you even buy them. In the changing room, check that you're properly covered up by leaning over (Does the top drop open, or does the skirt or dress lift too high in back?), raising your arms (Does the top or dress lift too high?), and sitting down (Do the pants show part of your backside, or does the skirt move too far up your legs?). Also check that the clothes don't fit too tightly. Look at more than just style and color—try to imagine what other people

see when they look at you. Take along an honest friend who can help you stay on the right track.

BEFORE YOU LEAVE THE HOUSE, MAKE SURE THAT . . .

 your zippers and buttons are done up.

 your clothes aren't dirty or too wrinkled.

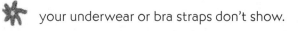 your clothes aren't see-through in the light.

 your underwear or bra straps don't show.

What's Happening to Me?

What to Expect

You've probably already noticed changes happening in your body in the last couple of years. This time of changes (*puberty*) happens to everyone—girls *and* guys—but not exactly in the same way or at the same time. Sometimes it can feel kind of awkward talking about this stuff, so here's some basic information for you. Knowing what to expect makes anything seem less scary or weird!

 Your breasts will start growing soon (if they haven't already). You may feel uncomfortable at times, but this will get better once you're more developed. If you don't already, you may need to start wearing a bra soon.

You'll start to see hair in places you didn't have any before (especially your underarms and pubic area). You'll also start producing more sweat, so . . . time to get some deodorant!

You'll get taller and maybe start putting on weight around your hips and thighs. That's normal. Just stay active and eat right.

You may start noticing white or yellow stains (called *discharge*) on your underwear. This is normal, unless you have itchiness or there's a bad smell, which could mean you have an infection. Discharge is a way for your body to clean itself out.

✳ Your period will start soon. Most girls get their first period around age twelve, but you could start earlier or later. You may have cramps or some pain before your period. When you find red spots or a bit of blood in your underwear, that's probably what it is. Let your mom or another woman you trust know, and she'll give you pads or tampons to protect your clothes.

✳ Your skin may become oilier and produce pimples. Keep your skin as clean as you can, but wash gently so you won't irritate it.

✳ You may become more emotional and sensitive. If you find yourself getting upset or feeling sad more than you used to, remember that you're going through changes. Go easy on yourself . . . and give other people a break too! Ask God to help you control your feelings.

You're on Your Way!

You're not a little girl anymore, but you still have a long way to go before you're a woman. On the path below, near "young girl" draw a little stick figure of yourself walking toward "woman." Then, in the space along the path, write a short prayer telling God how you feel about the changes you're going through.

young girl   woman

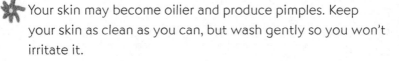

21

You may go through puberty without any problems . . . or you may struggle with many awkward moments. Either way, remember that God—your Designer—created your body. He knows what you're going through, and He will help you all along the way! You can talk to Him about *everything* without feeling embarrassed. Check out these verses for more encouragement.

January 22—Psalm 139:13-16
How do these verses make you feel about your body and how God designed it?

January 23—1 Timothy 4:12
Sometimes this stage of your life may feel awkward. What encouragement does this verse offer about the positive influence you can be while you're young?

January 24—Psalm 103:13-18
I can trust God to get me through my tween years because . . .

January 25—Psalm 34:18-19

What do these verses tell you about the difficulties you may face—now or in the future?

January 26—Romans 5:3-4

While your body develops, your character must also develop. What kind of character should people see in you?

January 27—Matthew 10:29-30

How much do you think God cares about the things you're going through?

January 28—Psalm 42:5

When I feel discouraged or confused by the changes I'm going through, I can . . .

Puberty . . . and Caterpillars!

When you were little, did you ever play with a caterpillar or watch a colorful butterfly? Caterpillars are usually cute and funny, like little kids, and butterflies may remind us of pretty and graceful women. But have you ever watched a caterpillar turn into a butterfly? When it has finished developing inside its chrysalis (sometimes called a *cocoon*), the adult butterfly sheds its covering and comes out with its wings folded tightly against its body. It then pumps blood into the wings until they expand and are ready to fly. It's an awkward, uncomfortable, and not very pretty process.

That's what puberty can feel like at times. Just remember the beautiful butterfly that comes out of the cocoon and trust that you, too, will get through puberty with your own special beauty!

You Are What You Eat

Silly Saying

"Vegetables are a must on a diet. I suggest carrot cake, zucchini bread, and pumpkin pie."

Garfield the Cat (Jim Davis)

Fun Food Facts

- Most strawberry milk shakes contain about fifty artificial ingredients to give them a "strawberry" taste!

- Red peppers have more vitamin C than oranges do.

- Tomatoes and green beans are actually fruits, not vegetables.

- Carrots are good for your vision.

- Americans eat more potatoes than any other vegetable.

- If you're between the ages of nine and twelve, you should eat at least five servings of vegetables every day.

Eat Healthy!

When people weigh much more than they should, doctors call that *obesity*. Obesity has become a very big problem in North America, especially for those in the nine to twelve age bracket. Too much junk food, not enough nutritious food, and not enough exercise can make you gain a lot of weight, which can cause serious health problems.

There's another big problem, though. Because many young girls are afraid of getting fat, they pick up other bad—and very dangerous—eating habits. For example, they may starve themselves, or they may eat too much and then purge (vomit) to get rid of what they ate. These eating disorders are so dangerous that some girls die if they don't get help! (Note: If you think someone you care about has an eating disorder, talk to a trusted adult or a nurse. They can give you advice or a helpful Web site or phone number for more information.)

The best way to stay healthy (not too fat but not too skinny) is to eat healthy food throughout the day. That means three good meals plus two *healthy* snacks every day. Don't go on a diet without the guidance of a doctor!

Dos and Don'ts

In the spaces provided, write down some good eating habits that you will start . . . and some bad ones you will drop!

Dos	Don'ts
eat more vegetables	skip breakfast
skip seconds of dessert	pour butter on popcorn

Getting good nutrition and eating regular meals help your body develop properly. In the same way, reading your Bible every day feeds your soul. You can't grow as a Christian if you don't get enough spiritual "food." Make sure you give your soul more of the good stuff—and less of the "junk food" that we sometimes get from TV, the Internet, movies, and magazines.

January 29—Matthew 5:6

What kind of hunger does the Bible promise will always be satisfied?

January 30—Psalm 42:1-2

How do these verses make you feel about your relationship with God?

January 31—Matthew 6:25-27

Explain what these verses mean to you.

February 1—Psalm 34:8

What do you think it means to "taste" God's goodness?

February 2—John 6:35

What kind of hunger is Jesus talking about in this verse?

....

February 3—Psalm 107:8-9

Dear God, I thank You for . . .

....

February 4—1 Corinthians 6:19-20

What changes do you think you should make in the way you eat so that you can honor God with your body?

....

....

Save Your Smile!

Don't forget that good eating and drinking habits don't just keep your body healthy and your weight under control . . . they also help your teeth stay in good condition! For example, be careful about drinking too much store-bought lemonade and iced tea. Studies show that they cause ten times more damage to your teeth than soft drinks do! (The best thing to drink? You guessed it: water!)

Say No, Stay Sober
Reasons to Resist

As a girl growing up today, you may face a lot of pressure to smoke, try drugs, and drink alcohol. You may know these things are bad for you, but do you know why? Understanding some of the effects of these substances may help you say no when you're in a tough situation.

When you drink alcohol, you risk . . .	When you do illegal drugs, you risk . . .	When you smoke, you risk . . .
getting sick	losing your ability to do well in school, sports, and other activities	getting gum disease, stained teeth, and more cavities than normal
gaining weight		
not being able to think clearly	losing your ability to make good decisions	smelling bad and having bad breath
not seeing clearly	becoming depressed or cranky	getting dry, yellow, smelly, and wrinkled skin
losing your memory		
blacking out	not being able to sleep well	weakening your bones and muscles
doing embarrassing things	losing or gaining too much weight	getting sick and having coughs that take a long time to go away
getting into trouble		
getting into a serious accident	looking sick or tired	causing damage to other people through secondhand smoke
being abused if you are too drunk to protect yourself	damaging your brain, heart, and other important organs	
		damaging your lungs
damaging your brain, heart, and liver	getting really sick or dying (many drugs are like poison)	getting cancer (in your lungs, mouth, or throat) or heart disease
dying if you get alcohol poisoning		

Sometimes people smoke, use drugs, or drink alcohol to help them forget about problems in their lives and relationships. They don't realize that these habits actually create bigger problems. God wants us to turn to *Him* when we're hurt or scared. It's also important to understand that all three of these habits are addictive, which means they are very hard to stop once you start . . . and they start to cause damage even *before* you're addicted.

Use Your Brain!

Here are some tips on how you can keep yourself free of drugs, alcohol, and cigarettes:

- Choose good friends. People who use drugs usually want to fit in with the cool crowd and don't feel good about themselves.
- Stay busy with healthy and fun activities.
- Don't be afraid to confidently say no when someone offers you something that's bad for you.
- Leave an event or activity where there are drugs or alcohol, or ask someone to come and get you.
- Ask for help from an adult or a good friend if someone keeps pressuring you.
- *Never* get into a car with a driver who has been drinking alcohol.
- Don't believe that you can stop whenever you want to. It's not that easy!
- Pray and ask God for His help and protection.

You only have one body and one brain. God expects you to take good care of them. After all, He created them, so they belong to Him! Not only that, but He loves you very much and wants you to enjoy the life He has planned for you. You can't do that if you're ruining your health and your relationships because of addictions to drugs, cigarettes, or alcohol. Let's see what the Bible says.

February 5—Proverbs 20:1
According to this verse, who is not wise?

February 6—Ephesians 5:18
What does this verse tell you about using alcohol to feel good?

February 7—Proverbs 23:29-30
What happens to those who become addicted to alcohol?

February 8—Psalm 86:1-7
Dear God, when I face pressure to try drugs or other harmful things, please . . .

February 9—Deuteronomy 30:11-16

How do these verses make you feel about the way God expects you to live?

....

February 10—Galatians 5:16-18

How can the Holy Spirit help you when you're facing a difficult situation?

....

February 11—Romans 7:21-25

When I struggle between doing wrong and right . . .

....

....

"But My Parents Drink Wine!"

Illegal drugs and smoking are bad . . . for *everyone*. Alcohol can be a trickier subject for some people. It is definitely harmful for children and teenagers because their bodies are still young and developing, but many adults can have a glass of wine or a beer without a problem, and the Bible doesn't forbid this. However, the Bible does make it very clear that we shouldn't become drunk or addicted to alcohol. Remember that it's not even legal to drink at your age, so as a follower of God, you know that this isn't even an option for you right now. Ask God to help you honor and obey Him in everything you do.

Run the Race!

Who Me? Sports?

What do you think of when you hear the word *exercise*? Soccer practice? Sit-ups? Running around a track? In-line skating? You probably know how important it is to get plenty of exercise, but those activities may not excite you very much.

Are you a strong athlete or good at sports? That's great! You're already ahead of the game. But what do you do if you're not? Believe it or not, there are lots of really fun things you can do for exercise.

SOME IDEAS TO GET YOU STARTED:

- play jump rope with your friends (or alone)
- go swimming
- climb a tree
- help with a building or painting job
- plant a garden
- learn to skateboard
- walk your dog (or a friend's dog)
- wash a family member's car
- build a snowman
- go bowling

Did You Know . . . ?

 The average American under the age of eighteen is inactive for 75 percent of the time she or he is awake. That means you probably move for less than four hours every day!

 The average American under the age of eighteen spends only *twelve minutes a day* in a vigorous physical activity.

 In Canada, only 30 percent of girls between the ages of five and twelve are physically active.

Corny Sports Jokes

See if you can get your friends to groan and roll their eyes with these silly riddles!

Q: Why is basketball such a yucky sport?
A: Because everyone dribbles on the floor!

Q: What do you call a boomerang that doesn't come back to you?
A: A stick.

Q: What is the hardest thing about skydiving?
A: The ground!

Q: Why was Cinderella kicked off the soccer team?
A: She ran away from the ball.

Regular exercise is important for your body. It keeps your heart strong, which helps to pump blood all through your body. Exercise makes your bones and muscles strong, and outdoor activities keep your lungs healthy. Exercise also sends oxygen to your brain and helps you think clearly. But physical exercise is not the *most* important thing we need! Did you know that to stay healthy and grow as a Christian you also need spiritual exercise and training? Let's take a look at what the Bible teaches about this.

February 12—1 Timothy 4:7-8
Why is exercise good for you? Why is being godly (doing the things God wants) even better?

February 13—Hebrews 12:1-2
A runner has to concentrate on the finish line during a race. How is that similar to our focus in the Christian life?

February 14—1 Corinthians 9:24-27
Ask God to help you "run the race" of being a Christian with courage and discipline.

February 15—Isaiah 40:29-31

My thoughts about how God helps those who trust Him:

....

....

February 16—2 Timothy 4:7-8

How is following God similar to winning a competition?

....

....

February 17—Acts 20:24

What is the most important goal in your life? What do you think it should be?

....

....

February 18—2 Peter 1:5-8

To grow strong as a Christian, I need to develop these qualities:

....

....

Learn from the Pros!

Athletes train every day for long periods of time. If you want to grow strong as a Christian, you'll need to set aside time on a regular basis to pray and read your Bible. No one makes it to the pros after just one practice!

 Professional athletes avoid junk food, drugs, and other harmful substances. Don't fill your mind and heart with the spiritual trash that is so common on television, on the Internet, and in magazines.

 They train with a coach. Find a mature Christian who can encourage you and help you grow as a Christian.

 They often practice with other athletes. If you don't have any good Christian friends, ask God for some. Get to know people of all ages at your church.

 They don't give up! Some days are hard, but God will help you get through them. Ask for His help every morning when you wake up.

Section 2

YOUR RELATIONSHIPS

Although friendships and families
sometimes get a little crazy, God designed you
to have relationships . . .
and He can help you enjoy them.

The Mysterious World of Boys

Who Are Those Strange Creatures . . . and Why Am I Starting to Like Them?

What does it *really* mean have a crush on someone, to have a boyfriend, or to date someone? And what's the right age to start? The best people to talk to about those questions are your parents, but here are some thoughts:

 Don't feel weird if you like a boy or think he's cute. That's perfectly normal! Just try not to be someone you're not around him. Be yourself. And be a friend.

 Be careful about starting a serious relationship or jumping into things too fast. Your feelings—and the boy's feelings—will get hurt later if the relationship doesn't last. Remember this even when you're older and thinking about marriage.

Concentrate on being friends. If you try to be girlfriend/boyfriend, you may end up making some foolish mistakes, such as becoming physically intimate too soon or even pushing away good friends because you're too busy with this new relationship.

Don't get physical with boys—no hitting, poking, pinching, tickling, holding hands, hugging, or kissing. Some of those things are good at the appropriate time and in the right relationship, but not yet. A good way to make sure boys treat you respectfully is to show them respect too.

 Don't rush. You have your whole life ahead of you to get involved with the right boy God will bring into your life at the right time. Pray that God will help you to trust and obey Him.

Give Them a Break

Sometimes the differences between guys and girls keep us from getting along with each other . . . or make us really curious about each other!

But guys and girls have things in common too. That's because God—our Designer—created all of us. Guys sometimes act tough, but believe it or not, they have feelings too! They get scared, they worry about how they look, they want other people to like them, and they need love . . . just like you do!

Guys also get confused when they like a girl, and they don't always know how to act. So don't get upset too quickly if a guy starts teasing you or acting strange around you. He may just feel nervous. Even if he's being rude or mean, try to be patient. Treat guys the same way you want to be treated. And ask God to show you the right way to be friends with guys.

DANGER SIGNS

You need to stop your relationship with a guy if . . .

 He tries to touch or kiss you, especially when you don't want him to.

He tells you to lie to your parents so you can go somewhere with him.

He treats you badly or embarrasses you.

He makes fun of your faith in God.

He says mean or rude things about your family.

It's better not to have a boyfriend for a long time—even until you're much older—than to let yourself get into bad situations. Know what else? It's not weird *not* to have a boyfriend, so don't feel bad if you don't have one yet. For now, try to enjoy all the blessings in your life and concentrate on school, your hobbies, your friends and family, and your relationship with God!

Maybe you're not ready for dating yet, but it's a good idea to start learning about how God wants you to treat guys and what the Bible teaches about relationships.

February 19—2 Corinthians 6:14

What does the Bible say about dating someone who isn't a Christian?

February 20—Romans 15:7

What kind of attitude should you have about the way guys are different from you?

February 21—2 Timothy 2:22

Dear God, when I feel tempted to push things too far or too fast with a guy, please help me to . . .

February 22—Philippians 4:19

If you're worried about not having a boyfriend, how can this verse encourage you?

February 23—Philippians 4:8-9

How can you make sure your thoughts about guys are on track?

February 24—Proverbs 31:30

What kind of girl should you try to become?

February 25—1 Timothy 5:1-2

How should you expect a Christian guy to treat other people, especially you?

Prepare for the Future

As you grow up and become a young woman, guys will start to watch how you behave around others, especially your family. They will also notice the relationship you have with God—your heavenly Father. If you work on having a loving and respectful relationship with your parents now, you will become the type of person others find easy to love and respect . . . especially the man you marry in the future. Pray and ask God to prepare you, even before you start dating!

The S Word

Get Serious!

Let's start this week by making one thing clear: God designed sex and He had a good plan for it. Sex isn't something dirty or embarrassing or gross or even funny. But you should understand that a lot of what you see and hear about sex—on TV, in songs, in ads, or at school—is far from God's design and purpose.

Although you still have to wait awhile before it's time to have sex (not until there's a wedding ring on your finger!), it's important for you to protect your heart and make wise decisions about sex . . . starting now! Many girls your age have no one teaching them about God's plan for sex, and they end up doing things that put them in danger or cause big problems in their lives.

Please read with a serious heart this week and ask God to give you understanding.

Keep It Pure

God made sex for two important reasons: To create babies . . . and for a married man and woman to enjoy each other's bodies. The rules are simple: You're only allowed to have sex with the person you're married to, and it has to be done with love. When we follow God's rules, sex is pure and beautiful.

Don't be fooled by people and messages that try to change the rules. Sex that doesn't follow God's rules becomes dirty and wrong . . . and even dangerous. Ask God to help you know what's true and right.

 46

HERE ARE SOME TIPS ON HOW TO KEEP YOURSELF PURE:

 Stay away from pornography (magazines, Internet sites, or movies that show or describe sexual activity). If you are curious about sex, talk with an adult you trust. Pornography will only confuse you and tempt you to have impure thoughts.

 Guard yourself. Showing off your body, flirting, or touching guys inappropriately will send a message that you're ready for sexual activity. Watch out for T-shirts or accessories with "sexy" messages on them too.

 Stop before you start! Many young people don't plan to have sex, but once they start kissing and touching someone, it gets hard to stop and they find themselves doing things they're not prepared for. Don't spend time alone with a guy, especially if you like each other. You may be tempted. And remember: Even sexual touching and oral sex are wrong outside of marriage. Don't go there!

 Don't chat with strangers online—and especially don't use a webcam or send photos or personal information! An unbelievable number of girls your age have been fooled by sexual predators (people who trick and then force others to do sexual things with them).

Pray, pray, pray! Ask God to protect your mind and heart and body. When you get married one day, you will feel really glad that you kept yourself sexually pure!

Note: Maybe you (or someone you know) have already messed up in this area. If so, God can forgive you. When you confess what you've done and ask for His help, He will make you clean again and give you a chance to start over.

You may be surprised to know that the Bible talks about sex . . . but it's not in the way you hear about it in movies or at school. The Bible teaches us about God's design for our lives and how we can enjoy His blessings when we obey Him. This week, compare what you learn in these Bible verses with what the world tells you about sex.

February 26—Ephesians 5:3
What does this verse tell you about the purity God expects from you?

....

February 27—Matthew 5:28
Sexual purity isn't only about keeping your body pure. What else does it mean?

....

February 28—Psalm 18:20-21
How does God treat us when we obey Him?

....

....

March 1—Job 14:4

What does this verse tell you about how you should choose the things you watch or listen to?

March 2—Psalm 51:10

Write this prayer in your own words:

March 3—Titus 2:11-14

I can depend on God to help me live a pure life because . . .

March 4—Colossians 3:5-10

Dear God, along with being sexually pure, please help me to also . . .

Have a Plan

In the space below, write down some ways that you can live in sexual purity according to God's plan, or some changes you may have to make in your life. You can also write down the names of two or three people you can ask to help you stick to these commitments.

From This Day Forward

A Promise . . . Not a Deal

If you've ever been to a wedding, you may have heard the bride and groom say something like this to each other:

> "I take you to be my lawfully wedded husband [or wife], to have and to hold, from this day forward, for better, for worse, for richer, for poorer, in sickness and in health, to love and to cherish, till death do us part."

That's a pretty big promise (also called a *vow*). If the man and woman really mean the words they say, they are making a promise to stay together no matter what happens . . . until the day they die! They're not saying, "I'll stay with you as long as you don't get on my nerves" or "I'll be your wife until I meet someone nicer and cuter" or "I want us to be together but only if you do whatever makes me happy." That would be making a deal—or a *contract*—with someone.

But in God's eyes, marriage is not a deal. It's a *covenant* between a man and a woman. That means making a promise because you love the other person, not because you want them to do something for you. That's why it's so important to be *very* sure about who you marry someday. Ask God from now on to start preparing you for that time.

Divorce Happens

Sadly, many of us have divorced parents. A lot of couples make "deals" with each other, and when they stop feeling happy in a marriage, they decide to end it. That's not what God wants, but it happens.

Often, the most difficult thing if your parents are divorced is trying to split your time between Mom and Dad.

 If you're in this situation, talk to God about it. He will give you the patience and strength to handle it. Pray for your parents, too, as the pain of divorce can take a long time to go away.

 If your parents are not divorced, pray for their relationship anyway!

 If you have friends with divorced parents, pray for those families. Show kindness to your friends . . . you never know when they may be feeling lonely or sad.

Crypto-Wedding!

The words below all have something to do with marriage or weddings . . . but you need to figure out the secret code! Once you solve a word, use those letters to decode the rest of the words. We've given you a few clues to get you started.

Clues: P = E, U = H, C = O, T = S, Y = C

YMDP _

JRCAPVT _

HVKNP _

VKLOT _

YUWVYU _

OVCCQ _

AUKBP NVPTT _

GVCQKTP _

QMKN CJ UCLCV _

VPYPGBKCL _

What about Me?

Maybe you're not thinking about marriage yet, but you probably
have some plans and hopes for your future. Isn't it encouraging to

SOLUTION: cake, flowers, bride, rings, church, groom, white dress, promise, maid of honor, reception

53

know that God determines our steps? (See Proverbs 16:9.) He's got a great plan for your life! While you wait to discover it, let's dream a little. . . .

What I think my life will be like . . .	in five years	in ten years
Where will I live?		
What will I be doing (school, work)?		
What will I look like?		
Who will my friends be?		
What activities will I be involved in?		

You may get married one day . . . or you may not! It's a good idea to start praying about your future. If you stay single, you can look for ways to serve God with the special life He has given you. If you want to get married and have a family, pray that God will show you what He wants for you too. He may help you meet the right Christian guy and prepare you to be a good and godly wife, or He may also give you a joyful and full life as a single person.

March 5—1 Corinthians 7:39

How is the last part of this verse similar to 2 Corinthians 6:14, which you read a couple of weeks ago? Why do you think the Bible is so serious about this teaching?

March 6—Matthew 19:3-9

What did Jesus teach about marriage and divorce?

March 7—Ephesians 5:22-24

How does God expect wives to treat their husbands?

March 8—Ephesians 5:25-33

How does God expect husbands to treat their wives?

March 9—Malachi 2:15-16

This is how God feels about the commitment between a husband and a wife:

March 10—Proverbs 12:4; 21:9, 19

This is what the Bible teaches me about being a wife:

March 11—1 Corinthians 13:1-7

What do these verses tell you about pure love?

Fact or Fiction?

Movies, books, and songs can give you all kinds of mixed-up ideas about love and marriage. You may end up with an unrealistic fairy-tale idea about what romance and marriage are like . . . or you may have a negative view about them. Make sure you're not letting your entertainment educate you about marriage. Instead, study the Bible, learn from the examples of mature Christians in your life, and don't be afraid to ask questions.

 56

Everyone Needs a Friend

Show You Care

Every day this week, try to do something from this list of ideas. Or use your own ideas! Then write down how you showed friendship in the table on the next page.

 Write a card telling your friend what you appreciate about her. Send it by mail!

 Call your local radio station and dedicate a song to your friend.

 Help a friend finish her chores so you can hang out together.

 Frame a cute picture of you and your friend and give it to her.

 Ask your parents if you can invite your friend's family over for a meal.

 At lunchtime, invite a girl you don't know very well to sit with you and your friends.

 Take time to pray for a friend, especially if she's going through some hard times.

Invite your friend to church or to a youth activity.

Plan a surprise party for a friend . . . for no reason except to make her feel special!

Day of the Week	How I Showed Friendship
Monday	
Tuesday	
Wednesday	
Thursday	
Friday	
Saturday	
Sunday	

Friendship Helpers and Harmers

There are lots of ways to keep friendships strong, but you can also easily ruin a friendship. In the list below, cross out the things that can harm relationships. Circle the things that make friendships great.

Apologizing

Gossiping

Having similar interests

Helping each other solve problems

Hugs

Hurting each other's feelings

Jealousy

Keeping promises

Kindness

Lying

Making others feel left out

Protecting each other

Respecting each other's parents

Selfishness

Sharing your stuff

Tempting each other to sin

Trusting each other

Yelling

Now draw a little check mark (like this: ✓) next to the things you need God's help with . . . and pray about these things right away!

59

Help! I Don't Have Friends!

Some people have a hard time making friends because they feel shy or left out, and others in the group haven't given them a chance. If you find yourself in this situation, try some of these ideas:

- Don't sit at home feeling sorry for yourself! Get involved in different activities that interest you so you can meet new people.

- Remember that you can have friends of different ages. Try to get to know younger kids as well as adults.

- Be friendly, smile, and show kindness. People who are worth having as friends will notice and appreciate it.

- Treat people the way you want to be treated.

- Take good care of yourself. Don't worry about looking trendy or beautiful, but make sure your hygiene or bad habits aren't keeping people away.

- Talk with your parents or other adults you trust and come up with some more solutions together.

$\mathcal{No}$ one likes feeling lonely. God designed us to have relationships—not only so we can receive love and care, but also so we can encourage and care for others. The more you study your Bible, the more you will discover that Jesus set the greatest example of friendship for us . . . and He can be your best friend!

March 12—Ecclesiastes 4:9-12

Why is it good to have friends?

March 13—Proverbs 27:6, 17

Why should you not be afraid to sometimes disagree with a good friend?

March 14—Proverbs 13:20; 24:1-2

What kinds of friends should you stay away from? Why?

March 15—Proverbs 17:9

What this verse tells me about forgiveness and gossip:

March 16—Hebrews 13:5-6

What kind of friend is God?

March 17—1 John 4:7-12

Dear God, please help me to . . .

March 18—John 15:9-17

What did Jesus teach us about friendship?

The Perfect Friend

In the space below, describe your idea of what the perfect friend should be like.

Now try to be this kind of friend to others!

 62

Parents Are People Too!

Different Kinds of Parents

Some of us live with both a mother and a father. Some of us live with just one of them, or with a parent and a stepparent. Some of us live with grandparents or other relatives, or have been adopted into new families. Others of us may live in foster homes or with other types of guardians. Some of us have loving and caring parents; others don't.

Whatever your situation is, you can know that God watches over you with love and that *He* is always there to take care of you in His own special way. And no matter how difficult you find it to get along with your parents, the Bible teaches that it's important to always show respect and love. Even when things seem unfair, God can help you share His love with the adults in your life.

And the Daughter of the Year Award Goes to . . .

Do you appreciate the things your parents do for you? Or do you take things for granted and complain more than you say thanks? Imagine how great your parents would feel if you did things that really showed your love and appreciation!

Here are some suggestions to get you started. Can you think of some more ideas on becoming an award-deserving daughter?

 Do *more* than your chores. Give your mom a break sometimes by doing jobs around the house that she usually takes care of. Don't feel satisfied cleaning up only your own messes.

 Ask your parents about their day and if there's something you can pray about for them. It will make them feel good to know that you care.

 Surprise them with little things. Tuck a cheerful little note into your mom's purse or tell your dad a funny story while he's driving you somewhere.

 Do your best! When you work hard in school and put a real effort into whatever you do, you'll be doing your part to make your parents proud.

🌸 Try to get along with your brothers and sisters. It's hard for parents to hear their kids arguing with each other all the time.

🌸 Honor God. When you take time to read your Bible, pray, and go to church, you will become the kind of girl God wants you to be—and a great daughter, too!

🌸 Your ideas:

Living with One Parent or a Stepparent

It's common to live with a single parent, or one parent plus a stepparent . . . and it can be tough! You may have extra responsibilities, you may feel lonely at times, and you may not always get along with your stepparent (or his or her kids, if there are any).

Talk about it with someone—your parents, another relative, a teacher, or even a friend who is in a similar situation. If something is bothering you, don't keep it inside! Many problems have solutions . . . and for those problems that you can't seem to handle, trust that God will help you through them. Remember: He's your heavenly Father and He loves you more than you can imagine!

Do you ever think that, if you'd had the choice, you would have chosen different people as your parents? The truth is, God knew exactly who you needed and He gave you your parents—so it's important to be thankful for them! The Bible teaches us to obey, respect, and love our parents, even when it's difficult. This week, pray for your relationship with your parents to grow and become more loving. Remember: How you treat your parents can be a good example to your non-Christian friends!

March 19—Colossians 3:20; Ephesians 6:1

It's important for me to obey my parents because . . .

March 20—Psalm 27:10

How can this verse encourage someone who doesn't have good parents?

March 21—Proverbs 1:8-9

Dear God, please help me to appreciate . . .

March 22—Proverbs 10:1

What are some ways you can make your parents happy and proud?

March 23—Proverbs 19:26; 28:24; 30:17

What do these verses warn about?

March 24—Matthew 10:37-39

What do you think Jesus meant by these words?

March 25—1 Timothy 5:3-4

What should your attitude be toward your parents and grandparents?

Tell Me a Story!

Have you ever heard stories about your parents or grandparents when they were your age? They probably have some interesting experiences they can tell you about. Take a break from TV and the Internet once in a while and ask your parents, grandparents, or other relatives to share their stories with you.

If you enjoy writing, get a nice journal and write some family stories. One day you'll have a wonderful storybook that you can share with *your* kids!

Oh Brother! (and Sister)

Are You an Only Child?

You may think you should skip this week's devo if you don't have any siblings (brothers or sisters). Think again! You can think of the Christians you know—your own age or older—as your spiritual brothers and sisters. They belong to God's family, just like you do! The things we'll talk about this week will be useful to remember in your relationships with your Christian friends. And you can share what you learn here with friends who have problems with their own sisters or brothers!

Sibling Matchup

There are all types of brothers and sisters. Can you match the terms with their definitions on the next page?

Types of siblings	Definitions
 Half brother or half sister	When three, four, or five babies are born at the same time. These are also called "multiples."
Stepbrother or stepsister	When your family takes care of a child for a while because his or her parents can't.
Identical twins	When two separate eggs grow inside the mother and are born at the same time (two boys, two girls, or one of each). You can tell them apart because they don't have the same genes and don't look identical.
Fraternal twins	When you have one parent the same.
Triplets, quadruplets, or quintuplets	When a mother's egg splits and two girls or two boys with the same genes are born. You usually can't tell them apart because they look identical.
Foster brother or sister	When your family officially makes a child with different biological parents part of your family.
Adopted brother or sister	When one of your parents marries one of this boy or girl's parents.

Bible Brothers and Sisters

Can you match up these brothers and sisters from Bible stories? There are eight sets here. Draw a line from each name to that person's brother(s) and/or sister(s). (Hint: Some of them have more than one sibling in the list!)

Aaron	James	Cain	Mary
Abel	Lazarus	Jacob	Miriam
Andrew	Leah	John	Moses
Benjamin	Seth	Joseph	Peter
Esau		Martha	Rachel

Maybe you come from a big family with lots of siblings. Maybe you're the baby in the family. Maybe you're the oldest. Maybe you're the only girl. Or maybe you're on your own. Whatever your situation is, you can learn a lot from what the Bible teaches about families and other relationships. And remember: When you see the word *brother* in these verses, it's talking about sisters, too!

SOLUTION: Aaron, Miriam, and Moses (1 Chronicles 6:3); Abel, Cain, and Seth (Genesis 4:1-2, 25); Andrew and Peter (John 1:40); Esau and Jacob (Genesis 25:24-26); James and John (Mark 3:17); Joseph and Benjamin (Genesis 35:24); Lazarus, Martha, and Mary (John 11:1); Leah and Rachel (Genesis 29:16)

 70

March 26—1 Peter 3:8

What does this verse tell you about the kind of relationship you should have with your brothers and sisters?

March 27—Psalm 133:1

How do you think God feels when you get along with your brothers and sisters?

March 28—1 John 4:21

Dear God, please help me to . . .

March 29—1 John 2:9-11

How do these verses make you feel about the way you love your siblings?

March 30—Matthew 5:23-24

To worship God with a right heart, first I have to . . .

March 31—Genesis 45:1-5

What can you learn from Joseph's example of how he treated his brothers?

....

April 1—Luke 15:11-32

This story teaches me that if my brother or sister does something wrong, I should . . .

....

....

Getting Along

At one time or another, most of us have trouble getting along with our brothers and sisters. An older sister can seem bossy. A younger brother can annoy you. A baby sister may touch your things all the time. What do you do? Try these ideas:

 Take a deep breath. Speaking calmly will solve the problem much faster than yelling will.

 Make time for fun together. If you and your siblings spend lots of time together doing things you all like, you will have fewer things to argue about. And your younger brother or sister will think you're cool!

 Show respect. Treat your siblings the way you'd like them to treat you. If they tell you that something you're doing bugs them, stop it!

 Show understanding. Your siblings have feelings too and face some of the same tough situations you face. Give them a break when they get on your nerves. Maybe they're just having a bad day.

 Pray! Ask God to help you become the best sister you can be.

Who Knows You?

What's the Big Deal?

When you hear the word popular, you may think of people who:

- are good looking

- wear trendy clothes

- have a lot of money

- act confident

- are allowed to go to "cool" parties and concerts

- hang out with other popular people

Now think of the people you would most like to have as friends. How many of them fit the description above? It's natural to feel like you need to fit in with the popular crowd, and yet most of us realize that there are more important things to look for in a friend. For example, you may have similar interests and hobbies, or you may appreciate the person's sense of humor or personality.

If you don't choose your *friends* because of their popularity . . . then how important do you think it really is for you to be popular? Ask God to help you stop worrying about your popularity . . . and just enjoy the great relationships you already have!

Popularity vs. Reputation

Do you have a good reputation? Do people trust you because you always keep your promises and do what you say you will? Do they think of you as kind and caring? Do they admire you for how hard you work in school and how respectful you are to your teachers and parents? Do they come to you when they need someone to talk to? Can they see Jesus' love in you even if you don't tell them you're a Christian?

These qualities may not make you the coolest kid in your school—but they will give you a good reputation. People will want to be your friend because they see the real you . . . not your money, good looks, or nice clothes.

What do *you* want—popularity or a good reputation?

Character Code

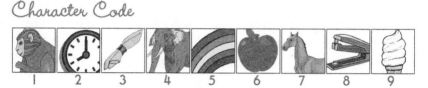

In the boxes below, write the first letter of each of the objects in the photo frames.

1	2	3	4	5	6	7	8	9

Using the code you just made, fill in the missing words below and you'll discover an important message from Proverbs 22:1 about having a good reputation.

A good ____ ____ ____ ____ is more desirable than great
        3   6   1   4

____ ____ ____ ____ ____ ____ .
5   9   2   7   4   8

Not everyone can be popular, but all Christians should have a good reputation. The Bible teaches us to live in such a way that people around us will not have anything bad to say about us. That doesn't mean that everyone will always respect you, but you don't have to worry if people don't like you . . . as long as you're doing your best to be a good friend and to honor God with your life. God's opinion of you matters more than anyone else's!

April 2—Proverbs 25:27

What does the second part of this verse tell you about trying to be popular?

April 3—John 12:42-43

How easily do you talk about your faith in Jesus? How much do you worry about what people will think of you?

April 4—Galatians 1:10

How do you think God feels when we try to please other people or get approval from them?

April 5—Matthew 23:11-12

Jesus' words in these verses teach me that . . .

April 6—1 Thessalonians 4:11-12

What are some ways you can earn the respect of others?

April 7—1 Timothy 5:24-25

Dear God, when people look at my life, please let them see . . .

April 8—Mark 10:31

What is the difference between Jesus' perspective in this verse and the attitude of the world around us?

Responsible Popularity

It's not *wrong* to be popular. If you're an outgoing girl who makes friends easily, others may think of you as popular. How does that make you feel? Do you act like you're better than others?

Popularity comes with responsibility. God can help you use your popularity for *good*. Look for opportunities to make a difference in your school or community. Help others who may need someone to stick up for them. Make friends with girls who seem shy. Start positive projects and activities that others can participate in.

You can use your natural leadership abilities in ways that please God!

Pushy People

What a Meanie!

Do you feel safe in your school and in your neighborhood? Every year, more and more students worry about being picked on by a bully at school or at a social activity. Sometimes bullying hurts on the inside, but other times it can become physically dangerous and scary.

THERE ARE DIFFERENT KINDS OF BULLYING:

 name-calling

 spreading secrets or lies about someone

 pushing

 hitting

 ignoring

 embarrassing

 discriminating (treating someone badly just because that person is different)

 forcing someone to give up money or other things that belong to her

throwing someone's things around

touching someone in a way he or she doesn't want

If you do any of these things, ask God to help you stop being such a bully!

If someone else does these things to you or to a friend, here are some things to do:

 Talk to a teacher or a parent and ask for help.

 Try to always stick with other friends. It's harder for a bully to bother a group.

 Try not to act upset. A bully will stop bothering you if he or she thinks you don't care.

 If possible, don't fight back. It usually makes things worse.

If you're really scared, give the bully what he or she wants. Your safety is more important than your stuff.

Act confident!

Remember this: A lot of bullies act the way they do because they don't feel good about themselves and think that picking on other people will make them feel better. Try praying for the bullies you know!

What Would You Do If . . .

. . . your friend took some candy from a store without paying?

a) Take some too, since she didn't get caught.

b) Pretend you didn't notice.

c) Tell her she should put it back because stealing is wrong.

. . . the other students in your class started making fun of your substitute teacher?
a) Laugh and misbehave too.
b) Sit quietly.
c) Try to get them to stop.

. . . your friends want you to skip class with them?
a) Go with them.
b) Tell them you want to but you are afraid of getting in trouble.
c) Tell them it's wrong and you'd rather go to class.

If you answered mostly A, ask God to help you make better choices and to say no to peer pressure.

If you answered mostly B, ask God to give you more courage to stand up for what's right.

If you answered mostly C, you're doing well! Pray that God will help you to continue making good choices.

You may not realize it, but your peers—other people in your class or age group—have a lot of influence on you. They may try to get you to act or dress or talk a certain way, to go places you know you shouldn't, or to do things that go against what God teaches. How can you keep yourself from giving in to peer pressure? These Bible verses will help you.

April 9—Proverbs 1:10-16

What does the Bible say to do when people tempt you to sin?

April 10—Proverbs 16:29

Why should you stay away from people who are violent or mean?

April 11—1 Corinthians 10:13

When you feel pressured to do something wrong, what does God promise you?

April 12—James 1:2-4

I can be thankful even when others treat me badly because . . .

April 13—James 1:5-6

What should you do when you feel confused or worried in a difficult situation?

 82

April 14—James 4:7-8

Dear God, please help me stay near You all the time so that . . .

....

....

April 15—2 Peter 2:9

Why should you trust God when you face peer pressure or bullying?

....

....

What's Bugging You?

In what ways do you feel pressured or bullied by other students? Write down what the Bible verses above taught you about how to deal with difficult situations like this.

....

....

....

....

....

....

....

....

....

....

Section 3
GROWING UP

The future may look like a big question mark, but learning and following your Designer's plans will make the journey a great adventure!

Feeling Dizzy?

Aaargh!

You're at a wonderful age because you're starting to experience so much more in life than you ever have before. Also, as we talked about in January— "What's Happening to Me?"—your feelings and emotions are growing and becoming more sensitive. That means that although you'll have many happy moments, you will also go through times of sadness, fear, excitement, anger, impatience, and lots of other feelings. You may even have moments where it seems you feel *nothing!*

You're normal. You *can* cope with your feelings, especially when you ask God for help. Ask Him each morning to help you control your emotions—most of all the negative ones. You can't always control how you feel, but you *can* control what you do about those feelings.

The Roller-Coaster Ride

Throughout each day this week, pay attention to all the different emotions you feel. As often as you can remember, put a check mark (✓) in the chart on the next page next to a feeling whenever you experience it. There is room at the bottom for other emotions you may want to add. At the end of the week, you may be surprised to see how many different feelings—ups and downs—you went through!

I felt . . .	This many times . . . (✓)
Angry	
Annoyed	
Ashamed	
Disappointed	
Excited	
Happy	
Hateful	
Hurt	
Jealous	
Loving	
Nervous	
Proud	
Relieved	
Sad	
Scared	
Shocked	
Sorry	
Sympathetic	
Worried	

Extra: If you've got time, take a piece of paper and write down what happened every time you experienced a noticeable emotion. Why did you feel the way you did? How did you behave? What would you do differently next time?

 88

Other People Have Feelings Too!

Don't you hate it when you're having a miserable day and your friends are being silly and loud? Or how about when you get excited about some great news—and no one else seems to think it's such a big deal? You may think, *What's wrong with them? Don't they understand how I feel?*

Just think . . . others go through the same thing! The waitress who didn't smile when she gave you your burger may feel upset about a family member who is sick. Your best friend may not feel like talking because of a difficult situation at home. Or your little sister may act excited about something you think is silly.

Practice this feeling: *empathy*. That's when you can almost feel whatever the other person is feeling. Ask God to give you a loving and understanding heart so that you can support other people, no matter how they feel. When you do this, you will probably find that others start caring more about your feelings too!

When God designed you, He gave you the ability to feel different emotions. Knowing that you were created in God's image should reassure you that He understands the feelings you experience. Of course, God doesn't sin and He doesn't struggle with confusing emotions like we do, but He knows what it's like to feel angry or hurt or joyful. This week, talk to God about your feelings. Even when no one else understands you, He will!

April 16—Philippians 4:4

How do you think you can rejoice always—even when you don't feel happy?

April 17—Matthew 11:28-30

Dear God, thank You that when I feel down I can . . .

April 18—Ephesians 4:26-27

How should you deal with angry feelings?

April 19—2 Corinthians 7:8-10

It's okay to feel guilt or sadness sometimes because . . .

April 20—2 Corinthians 1:3-4

How can we share God's comfort with others?

April 21—James 5:13

What are some good ways to express our feelings?

April 22—Psalm 34:15-18

How do these verses make you feel?

Feelings Come and Go

Sometimes people make quick decisions depending on how they feel at that moment—and they later regret it. Remember that you can't always trust your feelings. They can come and go based on how you're feeling physically (for example, tired, sick, or energetic) or what's going on around you. Always check with your brain, too, and make sure you understand the situation. Ask an adult or a trusted friend for help if you need to. And don't forget to pray! God is always ready to help, at any time.

Dream On!

From Nightmares to Daydreams

There are a couple of ways you can think about the word dream. At night you may see "movies" in your head while you're sleeping—they can be long or short, funny or scary, and even just really *weird*! You may remember some of them clearly, while you forget others as soon as you wake up.

Dreaming can also be what you do while you're awake, when you're thinking about the future—things you want to do and people you want to meet—or when you're making up stories in your head. We call that daydreaming or fantasizing.

Research shows that people ages ten to twelve daydream most about two things: popularity and being rich . . . especially those in the United States and India!

What about you? Write down some of *your* favorite dreams:

Nighttime dreams	Daydreams

 92

Ask your friends about their dreams and see how they compare with yours.

Caution!

Several Bible stories tell us about how God sent people important messages through their dreams. You may wonder if some of your dreams have a special meaning. Of course, it's possible for God to help you understand or feel better about something through a dream you have, but be careful about trying to find messages in all your dreams. The examples in the Bible were very special situations, not common events.

You may meet people who say they can decipher your dreams, or you may see articles in magazines and books that give explanations to common dreams. The Bible warns us not to pay attention to these things. We'll talk about this some more in July ("Dangerous Stuff"), but for now you can read and think about Jeremiah 29:8-9. God tells us not to listen to the dreams of people who don't follow Him, "because they are telling you lies. . . . I have not sent them" (NLT).

Where Do Dreams Come From?

Ever wonder why you see dreams at night? Well, scientists still haven't completely figured that out! What they do know is that while you sleep, there is a period of time called REM, which stands for "rapid eye movement." During this stage of sleep, your brain becomes active, and that's when you dream.

Isn't it cool that God created us in such a wonderful and mysterious way that even the smartest scientists can't understand everything? Take a moment to thank God for being your awesome Designer!

No matter what you dream about, you can trust that God's plans for your life are much better than anything you could imagine for yourself! At times you may find yourself worrying about the future or thinking that God won't give you something you really want. As you'll see in some of this week's verses, if you put your faith in God, you can feel joy and satisfaction in any situation, because your heart and mind will want the same things God does!

April 23—Psalm 37:3-7

What are five things this passage tells you to do to receive God's blessings in the future?

....

....

April 24—Proverbs 28:19

Why should you be careful about spending too much time fantasizing or daydreaming?

....

....

April 25—Ecclesiastes 5:3; 1 Peter 5:7

Sometimes we have anxious dreams when we have a lot on our minds. What can you do before going to sleep if you're worried about something?

April 26—James 4:13-14

Dear God, please help me not to be confident in my own plans and dreams because . . .

April 27—James 4:15-17

What attitude should you have about the future?

April 28—1 Corinthians 2:9

How do you feel knowing that God has plans for your future?

April 29—Proverbs 4:18-27

These are some of the things I need to do if I want a bright future:

Dear God . . .

In the space below, write out a prayer to God, telling Him about your dreams and asking Him to help you trust Him with your future.

School Daze

Common Ground

Whether you go to a large public school, attend a small private school, or are homeschooled, you probably have some things in common with other students your age. Sure, you may have different experiences—some find their studies really difficult, while others are honor students; some are really popular, while others have difficulty making friends—but we all face similar challenges at one time or another. You may have teachers who are difficult to get along with, classmates who annoy you, assignments that stump you, or disagreements with your parents about activities you want (or don't want!) to participate in.

Just remember that you're not alone. Whenever you're going through a hard time, you can be pretty sure that thousands of other kids understand what you're feeling!

Puzzled by School?

Look up the verses next to each row of squares on the next page. Try to find the key words related to education that fit into the puzzle. (You may want to use the New International Version so the words match up.)

Reference											
Psalm 119:7							**E**			
Psalm 139:6							**D**			
Ezra 7:10							**U**			
Matthew 22:36							**C**			
Proverbs 3:5							**A**			
Luke 6:40							**T**			
1 Kings 4:30							**I**			
Jeremiah 30:2							**O**			
Proverbs 24:32							**N**			

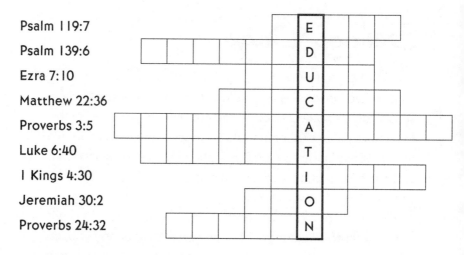

Cheating Is for Losers!

It's also foolish. If you cheat on your homework or on a test, you will get a grade you don't deserve. And you won't have learned anything! Your school lessons are meant to prepare you for things you will need to know later in life. And if your friends find out that you cheat, they may not feel they can trust or respect you anymore. (Remember, too, that a good friend will never ask to copy your work. Even if you're not the one copying, it's still cheating!)

Copying someone else's work or sneaking answers into class aren't the only ways people cheat. *Plagiarism* is when people copy information they've found on the Internet or in books and pretend they wrote it themselves. Even if they change some words into their own, it's dishonest and it's not fair to whoever wrote it in the first place.

If you want to use a sentence you found because it will help explain what you're writing, make sure you also say where you got the information. Give the name of the writer and the title of the book or Web address where you found the information. That's called giving proper credit to your source. Ask your teacher to tell you more about this.

Don't cheat, because God says not to—it's a sin! Cheating is a form of dishonesty, and God wants us to be fair and truthful in everything we do and say.

Top Ten Ways to Do Well in School

You may not be the top student in your class or even on the honor roll—every girl has different abilities. It's important to do your best, though, and work hard. The more you learn in school, the more opportunities you will have later when you want to go to college or find a good job. The hard work you do now will prepare you to manage bigger challenges in the future!

1. Get enough sleep every night, and eat a healthy breakfast every morning.

2. Each night before bed, get all your stuff ready for the next day.

3. Dress neatly but comfortably so you can concentrate on your classes . . . not on what you're wearing!

4. Keep your locker or desk clean so that you don't lose a book or homework . . . or find a smelly sock one day!

5. Be friendly to your classmates, but don't fool around with your friends during class time.

6. Respect your teachers, your principal, and the rest of your school staff.

7. When you don't understand something, ask!

8. Do your homework as soon as you get home from school—no watching TV until you're done!

9. When you get homework that's due in a week, don't wait to start it until the night before you have to hand it in. Get working on it right away! Same goes for studying for a test.

10. Pray every day, asking God to help you work hard and understand what you learn.

NOTE: If you're homeschooled, a lot of these tips will work for you, too! Think about how you might change the ones that don't fit . . . and then follow your own advice!

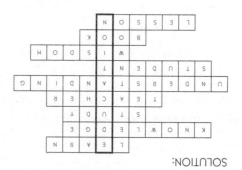

SOLUTION:

$\mathcal{A}$ good education is important, but did you know that intelligence does not equal wisdom? The Bible says that how much you know in your head isn't what makes you good or important. A wise person understands how to use what she has learned to make good decisions, to do what's right, and to please God. This also means that you shouldn't look down on someone who may not seem as smart as you!

April 30—Proverbs 9:10
How can you start to get wisdom?

May 1—James 3:13
How can people tell if you are wise?

May 2—James 3:14-16
What kinds of behaviors show that someone is not wise?

May 3—James 3:17-18
I want to have the wisdom that God gives because . . .

May 4—Proverbs 3:5-8

What will happen if you trust in God instead of your own knowledge?

....

May 5—Psalm 37:30-33

Why do you think it's important to try to do what's right in God's eyes?

....

May 6—Philippians 3:8

Compared to knowing Jesus, how important is everything else you learn? Ask God to help you know Jesus in an even deeper way.

....

A Lesson in Lexicons

Lexicon is another word for dictionary. There are some other important words on the next page that you will learn as you go through your school years. Look them up and see how many of them you already know!

Academics

Almanac

Antonym

Appendix (not the one in your body!)

Atlas

Bibliography

Encyclopedia

Glossary

Index

Reference

Research

Synonym

Thesaurus

Thesis

Priorities, Please!

What Do These Things Have in Common?

Each of these pictures represents a goal that you may aim for. We may think of goals as part of a sport or game, but we should have goals in life, too. You're at the perfect age to start deciding what's important in your life and, with God's help, doing your best to achieve those goals.

Anita DeFrantz, the first female vice president of the International Olympic Committee, once said, "Your goal should be out of reach but not out of sight." In other words, don't make your goals too easy (for example, beating your little sister at a game of checkers), but don't make them impossible either (for example, getting 100% or an A+ on every homework assignment or test this year).

Your Goals and Priorities

If you can't figure out what your goals are in life, start by looking at your *priorities*. These are the things that you give the most attention and time to. They will give you an idea of what goals you may have.

 104

In the boxes below, mark how important each priority is to you.

1 = the most important thing (choose only one)

2 = things that are very important

3 = things that are somewhat important

4 = things that are not important at all

Remember: Don't put down how you *want* to be or what you think the "right" answers are . . . just be as honest as possible.

- ☐ Being involved in my activities (sports, music, dance, etc.)
- ☐ Doing my chores
- ☐ Doing schoolwork
- ☐ Going to church
- ☐ Hanging out with friends
- ☐ Helping other people
- ☐ Trying to look good
- ☐ Praying
- ☐ Reading my Bible
- ☐ Shopping and having new stuff
- ☐ Spending time with my family
- ☐ Telling my friends about Jesus
- ☐ Watching TV
- ☐ Using the computer

What are some other priorities in your life? What changes do you think God wants you to make to your priorities and goals? Write them down here:

Everyone has goals and priorities. Some goals please God, and others don't. This week, take time to pray about the things you consider important, and ask God to show you if you need to rearrange your priorities or set new goals.

May 7—Psalm 42:1-2

Do you ever feel "thirsty" for God and for spending time with Him? How can you make that a greater priority in your life?

....

May 8—Matthew 16:24-27

How do you think Jesus feels about the order of your priorities?

....

May 9—Matthew 19:16-22

What can you learn from Jesus' conversation with the man in this story?

....

May 10—Proverbs 4:25-27

Dear God, as I try to achieve my goals, please help me to . . .

....

....

May 11—Proverbs 19:21
What should you remember as you set your goals and priorities?

....

....

May 12—Mark 12:28-34
These verses tell me that my priorities should be . . .

....

....

May 13—Matthew 6:28-34
What should you make your main goal in life?

....

....

Now . . . and Then
Goals can be short term (things you want to accomplish soon) or long term (for later in your life). For example, you may want to finish a painting you're working on (short term), and you may want to become a nurse when you're older (long term).

Write down your short-term and long-term goals and keep the lists in your Bible, on your wall, or in a journal or notebook. Check the lists once in a while and check off any goals you've achieved. Then have a mini-celebration, even if it's just by yourself!

If you're having trouble with one of your goals, try splitting it up into small steps instead of doing it all at once. It's okay to ask for help too!

What Do You Want to Do?

You're Not What You Do

Kids often get asked, "So, what do you want to be when you grow up?" Isn't it funny how we identify people by their jobs? For example, you may hear, "That man is a doctor," or "My aunt is a writer," or "The woman across the street is a professional swimmer." It's normal to say things like that, but shouldn't we look a little deeper into who people are, instead of at what kind of job they have?

So what about *your* future career? When you think about getting a job someday, consider what you like *doing* and what interests you . . . not what you want to *be*. Maybe this week's reading will give you some ideas about what you can do in the future!

Job Search

Can you find 20 occupations in the puzzle on the next page? They appear going down or across, and forward only (no diagonal or backward words). If you get stuck, look at the word list.

C E V H A A G T W T U D I R D
H H E H S R T D A O M U R E L
E M T A D T A A I U U L F P T
F V E F E I S A T R S I A H A
A H R I N S A R R G I B R O I
A E I O T T R H E U C R M T B
S T N R I I I R S I I A E O U
T L A W S F I I S D A R R G I
R A R A T H L E T E N I E R L
O W I A P I L O T R E A R A D
N Y A E N G I N E E R N E P E
A E N I L U A C T R E S S H R
U R B A K E R N T R N D E E R
T R T A T H C H E M I S T R I
R M I S S I O N A R Y I U L A

photographer	Farmer	builder	actress
pilot	lawyer	chef	artist
tour guide	librarian	chemist	astronaut
veterinarian	missionary	dentist	athlete
waitress	musician	engineer	baker

What's Out There?

One great thing about where you're at in life right now is that you can dream about what kind of job or career you want to have in the future . . . without the pressure of having to make a choice yet! It's wise to start thinking about what you might like to do, though. Take advantage of opportunities to explore different careers and read about your areas of interest. Some ways you can do that:

 Ask your parents and other adults you know about their jobs. Find out what they do and how they got into that type of work.

 Wherever you go, watch people working and see if you think their jobs interest you. Observe your bus driver, your dentist, the saleslady at your favorite clothing store, police officers in your neighborhood, your gym teacher, or anyone you see during your daily activities.

 Develop interests, try new activities, and volunteer. (You can check out the devos for October 15–21, "Send Me," for some volunteering suggestions.)

 Ask people you trust to tell you what they think your skills and talents are. Think about what you're good at—that may give you a clue about what kind of career to explore.

The Bible won't tell you what kind of job you should have someday, but it does give advice about finding out what God's will is for you, trusting Him with your future, and being the type of worker who pleases God and blesses others. Take time to pray about what direction He may want you to follow in your life.

May 14—Ephesians 6:5-8

This passage speaks about slaves and their masters, but the message is for workers and their bosses too. Whatever job you end up doing, how does God expect you to work?

May 15—1 Thessalonians 4:11-12

After reading these verses, I want to make these goals for my future:

May 16—Colossians 3:23

Dear God, when I get a job one day, please help me be someone who . . .

May 17—Proverbs 14:23

What does this verse tell you about laziness?

May 18—2 Thessalonians 3:10-12

What does the Bible say about people who don't want to work?

May 19—Matthew 9:35-38

What kind of workers do you think Jesus is talking about in these verses? Can you be one of those workers?

May 20—Romans 6:22-23

What can you receive as a gift from God that you could never work hard enough to deserve? Take a moment to thank God for His gift!

113

The Secret to Success

General Colin L. Powell once said, "There are no secrets to success. It is the result of preparation, hard work, and learning from failure." In other words, don't dream about being successful unless you're also willing to work hard at whatever you do.

It's also important to remember that you can't expect your career to make you happy someday. You may not always get to do what you like . . . but you can choose to like what you have to do!

SOLUTION:

 114

Dollars and Sense

Managing Your Money

In the United States, most twelve-year-olds get an allowance of about nine dollars per week. Of course, some don't get any allowance and others get much more than that. Those without an allowance may get money on birthdays or at Christmas or from small jobs they do, such as babysitting or mowing lawns.

Whether you have fifty cents in your piggy bank or fifty dollars in a bank account, it's time to start developing good money management habits. Many poor families around the world don't even have as much as your allowance to survive on. Make sure you appreciate what you have and use it thoughtfully.

A few tips:

 Don't just buy things you want *now*. Think about things you may want in the future, and have a plan to save up for them.

Money can't buy happiness. Never trust the feeling that says, *If I could just have this, I'd be happy.* New stuff may make you feel good for a while, but it can't fill your heart the way love can . . . especially God's love!

Learn to share. It feels good to help others. And who likes hanging around a greedy person, anyway? Once in a while, instead of buying something you want, get something you know your mom or best friend or little brother would like!

Currency Confusion!

Before we had dollars and cents, people traded things. They would pay with shells, tea, bags of rice, or even cows! It worked well for both people to exchange what they had for what they needed. But can you imagine carrying around a huge bag of beans or dragging a camel behind you whenever you went to the store? That's why people started making coins and paper money.

In the United States, Canada, and Australia, the currency used is dollars. *Currency* is what we call our money and how we measure it against other countries' moneys. Can you match the currencies below to their countries?

A—yen   1—India

B—peso   2—Israel

C—ruble   3—Brazil

D—shekel   4—United Kingdom

E—pound   5—Russia

F—real   6—Japan

G—rupee   7—Mexico

SOLUTION: A-6, B-7, C-5, D-2, E-4, F-3, G-1

Basic Budgeting

Not everyone uses a *budget* (a plan for managing your money), but it can really help people who have difficulty saving. Want to try making yourself a simple budget?

 116

First, decide how you will divide your money. Then, write down how much you will give away, save, and spend each week. Here are two examples below. (Remember: You don't *have* to spend all your spending money. You can save what's left over—or give it away!)

1. If you get $6 a week, you may decide to give 1/3 away (to your church or to a charity), save 1/3, and spend 1/3. Your budget would look like this:

Give away $2
Save $2
Spend $2
Total $6

2. From $10 a week, say you decide to give 10% as an offering at church, save 30%, and spend the remaining 60%. Your budget would look like this:

Offering $1
Save $3
Spend $6
Total $10

What do you think? Take a moment to ask for God's help in deciding what to do with your money. Talk it over with your parents, too!

My Budget

Offering   _____

Save   _____

Spend   _____

Total   _____

Note: If you want to, you can divide your spending budget into specific categories, such as clothes, music, candy, etc. Why spend $6 on candy when you could save some of that for a new CD once in a while?

James 1:17 says that every good gift we have comes from God. Unfortunately, we often complain when we don't have things we want . . . and we forget how much God has given us! This week, ask God to help you be a good steward (or manager) of the money He gives you. (Even when you work for it, it's still a blessing from Him!) It's important to save—without becoming greedy. With God's help, you can be smart and generous.

May 21—Proverbs 3:9
What should you do with your money?

May 22—Luke 12:15
How much of a priority should money be in your life?

May 23—1 Timothy 6:10
It's dangerous to love money because . . .

May 24—2 Corinthians 9:6-7
What attitude should you have when you give? Why?

May 25—Luke 11:42
It's important to give your offering to God, but what does God want even more?

May 26—Ecclesiastes 5:10

Dear God, please help me understand that money can't . . .

May 27—Mark 12:41-44

What can you learn from this poor widow's example?

The Highest Price

The Bible says that "you were bought at a price" (1 Corinthians 6:20). Did you ever think about what it cost Jesus to forgive your sins and save you from hell? He suffered and died a painful death on the cross because of His love for you and because He wants you to live with Him forever in heaven. Why not thank Him for that precious gift today? You can never pay Him back . . . but you *can* live for Him!

Life Is Short

Are You Ready?

You probably don't spend too much time thinking about getting old or dying, right? You're too busy enjoying life, going to school, exploring, hanging out with friends, and doing all the things you love to do! Old age and death may seem a long way off for you.

It's true that you won't be old for many more years, but any grandparent will tell you that the years go by quickly—the older you get, the faster time seems to pass.

What about death? Is that a long time away for you? There's no way of knowing that. Most of us hope we won't die until we're really old, but that's not always what happens. You probably know of children, teenagers, or young adults who have died . . . long before they got old. People can die from accidents, cancer or other diseases, suicide, or even murder.

But you don't have to be scared of dying! When you ask Jesus to forgive your sins and you faithfully live for Him, you can know that you will go to heaven when you die. Do you have that confidence today? If not, talk to God about it this week!

Getting Over Grief

As a Christian, you don't have to worry about what will happen to you when you die. But it's hard when someone else dies, especially if that person was close to you. The sadness you feel when someone dies is called *grief*. Even if this person was a Christian and you know he or she is in heaven, you will feel sad because you miss that person. It's like a certain part of you is gone.

Here are some suggestions that may help you when you experience grief:

 It's okay to cry. Don't feel like you have to hide your feelings. (Just make sure you don't hurt other people who are grieving by your actions and words.)

 Remember the person who died. Talk about him or her and share with others the good memories you have. Or write down your memories in a journal or a scrapbook. Include pictures if you have any.

 Talk to God about it. He understands and cares. It may be hard to believe, but the hurt you feel will not be this overwhelming forever. God can heal your heart.

What's It Like to Be . . . ?

Try to find people who fit into the age groups on the next page. Ask what they like the most and the least about their age. Ask what age they wish they could be. In the last row, write down your answers!

Age group 10 to 19   Name: ....

Like the most . . . .

Like the least . . . .

Wished-for age . . . .

Age group 20 to 29   Name: ....

Like the most . . . .

Like the least . . . .

Wished-for age . . . .

Age group 30 to 39   Name: ....

Like the most . . . .

Like the least . . . .

Wished-for age . . . .

Age group 40 to 49   Name: ....

Like the most . . . .

Like the least . . . .

Wished-for age . . . .

Age group 50 to 59   Name: ....

Like the most . . . .

Like the least . . . .

Wished-for age . . . .

123

Age group 60 to 69   Name:

Like the most . . .

Like the least . . .

Wished-for age . . .

Age group 70 to 79   Name:

Like the most . . .

Like the least . . .

Wished-for age . . .

Age group 80 or older   Name:

Like the most . . .

Like the least . . .

Wished-for age . . .

Your Answers   Name:

Like the most . . .

Like the least . . .

Wished-for age . . .

I_n the Old Testament, Methuselah lived to be 969 years old (see Genesis 5:27). Imagine trying to light candles for his birthday cake! Today the oldest living people may be around 120 years old, but we usually expect people to live only until about eighty or ninety. The Bible reminds us that life is short, so we have to live for God *now*. Don't wait until you're older. . . . It may be too late then!

May 28—Psalm 39:4-5

What do these verses say about how long life is?

May 29—2 Timothy 2:11

What do you think this verse means? How does this promise encourage you?

May 30—1 Timothy 5:1-2

Dear God, when I am with an older person, please help me to . . .

May 31—Titus 2:2-3

What kinds of attitudes and behaviors will God expect from you when you're older?

June 1—Isaiah 46:4
How does this verse make you feel about becoming old one day?

....

June 2—Philippians 1:21-24
How did the apostle Paul feel about living and dying?

....

June 3—1 Corinthians 15:55-57
Death won't "sting" or have power over me because . . .

....

....

What about Suicide?
You may wonder if someone who commits suicide can go to heaven. That's a tough question because only God really knows the condition of someone's soul just before he or she dies. It's important to understand, though, that committing suicide is a sin. You don't have the right to end anyone's life—not even your own. Your life is a gift from God, and you can trust Him, even in the most difficult situations. As you'll learn next week, God has the power to take care of *any* problem.

Section 4
YOUR SOUL

Get to know your Designer personally—and
discover the girl He created you to be!

Getting to Know God

Only God

Brennan Manning, a well-known Christian author, once said, "He is the only God man has ever heard of who loves sinners."

There are hundreds of different religions in the world, some of them completely different from Christianity, and some that seem similar. Some people don't believe in God at all; others believe there may be some kind of god out there (we say god with a small g when we're not talking about the God we learn of in the Bible), and some people worship many gods.

The amazing thing is that our heavenly Father is the only God who really *lives*. He talks to us, hears our prayers, forgives us, saves us, and loves us. We can have a relationship with Him! He even came down to Earth through the birth of Jesus and lived among human beings. Later He died on the cross to take the punishment that we deserve for our sins. No other faith or religion has a god who can do that!

Omni-Everything!

You may sometimes hear people describe God as being *omniscient, omnipresent,* and *omnipotent.*

Omniscient means "knows everything" (check out 1 John 3:20). Because God created the earth and everything in it, including human beings, He knows everything that has ever happened, everything that is happening right now, and everything that will happen in the future. He knows what you're thinking, how you feel, what you need, and what your dreams are. Sound scary? It shouldn't. You can feel comforted in knowing that God can and will take care of you because He's not only omniscient . . . He's also loving!

In what area of your life do you need to remember that God is omniscient?

Omnipresent means "is everywhere" (see Psalm 139:7-10). You can't find a single spot on this earth or in the entire universe where God doesn't exist. We can only go wherever our bodies go, but God is spirit and He can be everywhere at the same time! That's great news because it means He's always right there with you when you need Him. Omnipresent also means that God has always existed—and He always will!

What are some times when you need to remember that God is omnipresent?

Omnipotent means "all-powerful." God has the power to do anything He wants to do. He also has the authority to do whatever He wants to (see Matthew 28:18). That means there's nothing God can't do . . . and no one can tell God what to do! Isn't it great to know that He can help you through the most difficult situations— that He uses His omnipotence for your good?

Tell Him!

Write a letter to God and tell Him all the things you love about knowing Him—or ask Him to help you get to know Him better!

In the space at the bottom of the next page (or on a separate sheet if you need more room), write down questions you have about God. Ask your parents, pastor, youth leader, or Sunday school teacher if they know the answers. If they don't, ask God to help you to trust Him and believe anyway. You may find the answers later on . . . or only when you get to heaven! The important thing is to always try to know God more and more.

June 4—Romans 5:6-8
What do these verses tell you about God?

June 5—1 John 3:16-18
What can you learn about love from Jesus' example?

June 6—Matthew 19:26
What is an "impossible" situation you are facing right now? How does this verse encourage you?

June 7—Acts 17:24-29
Write down anything new you learned about God from these verses:

 132

June 8—Isaiah 40:28

What are some things people in our society don't understand about God?

June 9—Jeremiah 32:17, 27

How do these verses encourage you?

June 10—Psalm 23:1-4

Thank You, God, for . . .

So Many Questions!

Conversations with God

You've Got a Backstage Pass!

Think of your favorite singer, actor, or athlete. Imagine you have free tickets to see him or her at a big event. Now imagine you have a backstage pass and can join a special group of fans getting autographs. Can you handle it so far? How about this? The star you admire so much comes out to meet you, gives you his or her private cell phone number, and tells you that you can call anytime you want to talk!

Wow! How cool would that be?

Here's the amazing thing: We have that kind of "pass" from the God of the universe, but we don't use it very often! Did you know that you can talk to God at any moment, no matter what time it is or where you are? Isn't that more exciting than being able to talk to another human being? God, your Designer, loves you more than anyone else ever could, and He wants to spend time with you. Don't waste your backstage pass—go and talk to God right now!

Prayer Tips

Divide a notebook into three sections (or divide each page into three columns):

1. Things I'm thankful for
2. People to pray for
3. My own needs

Whenever you think of something that fits into one of those sections, write it down. Then pray about it right away. Later you can look back at what you've written and think about how God answered your prayers.

 Get a calendar with space to write on. For each day of the month, write the name of someone you can pray for, or anything else you think you should remember to pray about. Check the calendar each day and pray for that person or situation.

 Choose activities or chores that you do alone and make those special times to pray. For example, you can pray while brushing your teeth, taking your shower, washing dishes, folding laundry, walking the dog, or cleaning up your room.

 Remember that you're talking to a real person! That should help you pray in a more thoughtful and respectful way. Figure out ways to pray that help you focus on who God is: close your eyes, kneel, find a quiet place, choose a special chair, or go on a prayer walk.

God Always Answers

You may not get everything you pray for, but you can trust that God always hears and answers your prayers. If what you've asked for pleases Him, He may say yes. If He knows that what you've asked for will not be good for you, He may say no. And sometimes He may want you to wait a while before He answers.

Think of some things you (or people you know) have prayed about before. How do you think God answered?

Prayer request	Yes	No	Wait
_ _	☐	☐	☐
_ _	☐	☐	☐
_ _	☐	☐	☐
_ _	☐	☐	☐
_ _	☐	☐	☐

In the Bible, Jesus set the best example of praying. We read about how He would get up early in the morning and go to a quiet place to pray. He taught His disciples how to pray, and He invites you to pray too. God loves you and wants to bless you with good things. This week, before you read each Bible passage, take a moment to ask God to help you understand more about prayer.

June 11—Philippians 4:6
What does this verse teach you to do when you feel worried?

....

....

June 12—Matthew 6:5-8
What do these verses teach you about how you should pray?

....

....

June 13—Matthew 6:9-13

In this example of prayer, what kinds of things do you see that you can pray about too?

June 14—Matthew 6:14-15; Mark 11:24-25

If you want God to forgive your sins, what do you have to do first?

June 15—1 John 3:21-22

When can you feel confident that God will give you what you've asked for?

June 16—James 4:2-3

I think that sometimes I don't get what I've prayed for because . . .

June 17—1 Thessalonians 5:16-18

How often do you think you should pray?

Pour Out Your Heart

"God is great, God is good, let us thank Him for this food."
"Now I lay me down to sleep, I pray the Lord my soul to keep. . . ."

Have you ever heard kids say those prayers? Maybe you've said them yourself. What about the prayer in Matthew 6:9-13? Whether you're alone or at church, whenever you say prayers like these, think about the words—don't just repeat them. And remember that you can talk to God in your own words! When you pray, make sure your words come from your heart. They don't have to sound fancy. . . . They just have to be real!

What Is Worship?

God Deserves Your Praise!

Think about how you treat your favorite people and the things you happily do for them. Why do you enjoy spending time with your best friend? How often do you listen to songs by your favorite singers?

When we admire someone, we devote time to them . . . and we tell them about our feelings if we can. We should do the same with God.

God loves you more than anyone else will ever love you, and He has blessed you with everything you need . . . and then some! Most of all, He sent Jesus to die on the cross and be punished for our sins so that we can live forever with Him in heaven.

When you thank God for all He has done, and you take time to tell Him how wonderful He is, that's called worship. This week we'll look at some of the different ways we can worship God. Start thinking about how *you* can worship God!

Praise Puzzle

Use the chart on the next page to figure out the letters that go on the numbered dashes below. When you solve the puzzle, you'll find another great reason to worship God, from Psalm 13:6.

A	B	D	E	F	G	H	I	L	M	N	O	R	S	T	W
39	70	61	29	55	72	42	1	51	37	60	11	76	6	58	45
54	48	34	23	71	31	22	69	5	41	30	20	21	44	10	46
25	87	80	14	19	86	13	7	73	79	52	33	43	77	35	57
63	27	18	93	64	40	95	50	15	89	8	32	53	26	67	2
74	62	75	38	47	81	24	65	94	59	92	16	91	84	12	78
49	82	96	28	56	9	88	3	4	83	66	36	17	90	85	68

___/___ ___ ___ ___/___ ___ ___ ___/___ ___/___ ___ ___ ___/___ ___ ___ ___,/___ ___ ___/
1 2 3 4 5 6 7 8 9 10 11 12 13 14 15 16 17 18 19 20 21

___ ___/___ ___ ___/___ ___ ___ ___/___ ___ ___ ___/___ ___/___ ___/___ ___.
22 23 24 25 26 27 28 29 30 31 32 33 34 35 36 37 38

Unlimited Worship

What do you think of when you hear the word *worship*? For a lot of people, worship just means singing songs in church. God loves it when we sing to Him, but there are other ways we can show Him how much we adore Him.

Did you know that you can worship God anywhere, at any time, and in many different ways? There really is no limit to the ways we can worship God . . . because there is no limit to how wonderful He is!

Add some of your own ideas to this list of ways to worship:

 Make up your own songs to tell God you love Him—and sing them in the shower!

 Before getting out of bed each morning, think of five new things to thank God for (don't repeat yourself).

SOLUTION: "I will sing to the LORD, for he has been good to me."

 140

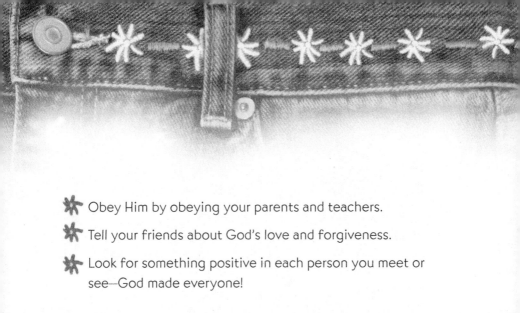

 Obey Him by obeying your parents and teachers.

 Tell your friends about God's love and forgiveness.

 Look for something positive in each person you meet or see—God made everyone!

The more you worship God, the closer you feel to Him and the more you get to know Him. The more you get to know Him, the more things you discover about Him that you want to worship Him for. Pretty soon, you may find yourself praising God more and more, even if it's just silently in your head! As you do this week's devotions, take extra time to worship God. It doesn't matter how . . . as long as it's from your heart!

June 18—Jeremiah 10:6-7

According to these verses, how much worship does God deserve?

June 19—Psalm 96:8-13

Dear God, I want to worship You because . . .

June 20—Mark 7:6-8

What kind of worship doesn't make God happy?

....

June 21—Psalm 24:3-5

Before I worship God, I should make sure that . . .

....

June 22—Nehemiah 9:6

What are some reasons God deserves praise? Add your own ideas too.

....

June 23—Psalm 63:3-7

How do you feel about the way you worship God after reading these verses?

....

June 24—Psalm 148

Write a short prayer, praising God in your own words:

....

....

Make It Private; Make It Public

Check out Psalm 35:18 and Daniel 6:10. What can we learn about worship from both of these verses?

_____

_____

_____

_____

_____

_____

_____

_____

_____

_____

_____

_____

_____

_____

_____

_____

_____

Look for opportunities each day to worship God—whether you're alone or in the middle of a crowd!

Read It . . . You Need It!

It's Alive!

If a friend asked you what the Bible is, how would you answer? Would you say it's a book that talks about God and Jesus? That it explains how to be a Christian and go to heaven? That it tells us how to live our lives? That it contains stories about people who lived a long time ago? That it says what will happen in the future?

All those things are true! But the Bible is much more than that. One amazing thing that makes the Bible so different from any other book is that it is alive! That doesn't mean it's like a human or an animal, but because God speaks to us through the Bible, it has real and wonderful power in people's lives.

Don't Know Where to Start?

Maybe you want to read your Bible but you aren't sure what to read or how to remember what you learn. Try some of these ideas:

 Read the New Testament first. The fourth book, John, is one of the books that tells the story of Jesus' life, so that's a great place to start. Pay special attention to chapter 3, which talks about God's love for the world.

 Keep a notebook nearby. Whenever you read from the Bible, write the date, what section you read, and what you learned. Copy down any important verses that you want to remember and read again later.

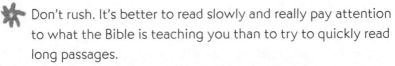

 Don't rush. It's better to read slowly and really pay attention to what the Bible is teaching you than to try to quickly read long passages.

 Make it a habit. The more often you read your Bible, and the longer the periods of time you read for, the more you will learn and understand. Should you give more time to God and His Word than you do?

 Memorize important verses, and they will come to your mind just when you need them.

Not So Old-Fashioned!

Some people think that because the Bible was written such a long time ago, it's not useful in our lives today. As you read it, though, you'll find that the stories and lessons are surprisingly similar to situations you face each day!

HAVE YOU EVER . . .

. . . wondered if your best friend would stick with you through a tough situation? Read about David and Jonathan's friendship in 1 Samuel 18–20.

. . . known you should do something but were scared? Read about Esther's scary adventure in Esther 2–9.

. . . felt like you weren't good enough for Jesus to care about? Read about Zacchaeus's encounter with Jesus in Luke 19:1-10.

. . . wondered whether God hears your prayers? Read about a time Elijah felt this way in 1 Kings 19:1-18.

. . . been tempted to think only of yourself? Read about how God blessed Ruth for being unselfish in Ruth 1–4.

There are many more wonderful stories in the Bible. See how many you can find!

Think of the Bible as a friend—as God's way of being right there with you, talking to you and teaching you important things you need to know. The devil may tempt you to do other things instead of reading your Bible, so take extra time this week to pray that God will help you get serious about reading His Word.

June 25—Psalm 119:105

Dear God, I thank You for giving me the Bible because . . .

June 26—2 Timothy 3:16-17

In your own words, what do these verses say the Bible is useful for?

June 27—John 20:30-31

Reading about the life of Jesus in the Bible helps me to . . .

....

....

June 28—Psalm 19:7-11

What are some ways the Bible can help you?

....

....

June 29—Psalm 119:11

How can studying and memorizing God's Word help you in your life?

....

....

June 30—James 1:22-25

Why is it not enough to only read the Bible? What else should you do?

....

....

July 1—Deuteronomy 4:2; Revelation 22:18-19

What does God say about trying to change the teachings of the Bible?

....

....

....

Don't Leave It on the Shelf

WOULD YOU EVER . . .

. . . carry around a closed umbrella during a storm?

. . . get a new computer and keep it in the box?

. . . walk around a strange city without looking at a map?

. . . try taking a bath while sitting in a mud puddle?

. . . find a treasure chest and use it as a bench without ever looking inside?

. . . buy a new outfit and never take it out of your closet?

Those ideas seem pretty ridiculous, right? Well, having a Bible and not reading it is even more foolish . . . but that's exactly what many people do. If you don't read your Bible every day, you're missing out on a lot: food for your soul, protection for your mind, directions for your life, advice for your problems, and much more!

Let's Get Together
Fellowship Puzzle

To see what the Bible says about going to church, find the hidden message in the puzzle below. Follow these instructions:

1. Cross out all the flowers.
2. Cross out all the foods.
3. Cross out all the months.
4. Cross out all the sports.
5. Cross out all the musical instruments.

ROSE	LET	PEANUT	JULY	US	TENNIS
BASEBALL	BANANA	NOT	PIZZA	AUGUST	SOCCER
APRIL	VOLLEYBALL	PIANO	PASTA	VIOLET	CHEESE
GIVE	DAISY	OCTOBER	UP	HOCKEY	JUNE
COOKIE	VIOLIN	LILY	MEETING	JANUARY	RICE
GUITAR	DECEMBER	DRUMS	TULIP	TRUMPET	TOGETHER

Write the leftover words here (Hebrews 10:25).

_____   _____   _____

_____   _____   _____

_____

149

Give and Take

If you feel the same way after church as you did before you got there, maybe you could be doing something more to make the most of your time there. It's important not only to get as much as you can out of the worship and fellowship (spending time with other Christians), but also to give—to share your talents, time, and money—as much as you can.

Here are some ways you can enjoy church . . . and bless the other people there!

 Bring along a notebook or journal each week to write down things you learn during the service. This will probably help you pay more attention to what the pastor says. If you don't understand something, write it down and ask your parents, the pastor, your youth leader, or your Sunday school teacher later. (Don't forget to write down the answer to your question too!)

 In your notebook, write down words from songs that help or encourage you, prayer requests you can pray for throughout the week, or special announcements you need to remember.

 Don't talk or walk around during the service.

 Volunteer to help in the nursery or the kitchen.

Treat the building and grounds with respect.

Talk to people you don't know very well, not just your friends.

Pray for your pastor and the other leaders as often as you can.

Have you ever tried building a campfire with just one stick? It may burn for a little while, but you won't have a fire—or very much heat—for long. A fire burns best when you have small branches and big logs crisscrossed with each other . . . not spread all over the ground! In the same way, Christians can't stay at home and expect to grow strong in their faith or be useful in serving God.

July 2—Psalm 27:4

Compared to the attitude in this verse, my attitude about going to church and worshipping God is . . .

July 3—Romans 12:4-8

What do these verses say about how important each person at church is?

July 4—Romans 15:5-6; 1 Corinthians 1:10

How do you think God feels when people in churches don't get along with each other?

July 5—1 Timothy 5:17

How should you treat the leaders and teachers in your church?

July 6—Colossians 1:13-14, 18

What do these verses tell you about who should receive the most honor in a church? Why?

July 7—1 Corinthians 12:27-31

God gives the people in a church different abilities and talents. How do you think He may want you to help in your church?

July 8—Acts 2:41-47

What can you learn from the example of the first Christians who got together as a church?

So, You Don't Go to Church?

If your parents don't go to church or you don't have transportation to get to one, that can make it difficult to get involved in a church. Pray that God will make a way for you to get to a good church where you can worship Him, learn about Him, be encouraged by others, and serve Him with your talents. Try talking to an adult you trust about your desire to go to church and ask if he or she can help you.

In the meantime, why not make a special time for God on Sunday mornings and have your own "church"? You could sing a couple of songs (or listen to Christian music), read your Bible, and pray. See if a friend or anyone in your family wants to join you. If you're taking time out to worship God, He will bless you and help you grow in your faith!

Got Any Fruit?

Picture This

Imagine two identical little figures, one named Joy and the other Peace. Joy happily dances and skips around the room. Peace lies down on the couch, stretched out comfortably and smiling. Joy and Peace are very similar but they act different. You could say that Joy is like Peace dancing and that Peace is like Joy resting!

Joy and peace describe the feeling deep inside that, even in sad or difficult times, everything is okay because God is in control. So how are they different? Joy sometimes feels like it's going to bubble out of us—like dancing! Peace feels like a comfortable calmness—like resting.

Just remember: When you invite God into your life, His Holy Spirit will give you peace and joy!

Memory Tip

After reading the Scripture given for Tuesday, try to remember the fruit of the Spirit listed in those verses. Here are a couple of tips that may help you:

1. The list of fruit can be divided into three groups of three. The first group is made up of one-syllable words: love, joy, and peace. The second group includes two-syllable words: patience, kindness, and goodness. And the third group contains three-syllable words: faithfulness, gentleness, and self-control.

2. Think of nine fruits that you like to eat and make each one symbolize one fruit of the Spirit. For example, apples can remind you of love, oranges can remind you of joy, and peaches can remind you of peace. In the space below, draw your fruits and label them with the fruit of the Spirit you chose for each one. Then, every time you eat one of those fruits, think about the fruit of the Spirit it represents. Ask God to help you develop that fruit in your life.

If you see pears on a tree, you know you're not looking at a banana tree. You won't find oranges on a vine. And you'll never see watermelons growing on a bush! As you will read in Matthew 7:16, people recognize a tree by its fruit. If you're a Christian, people should recognize God's character in your life. Things like dishonesty, rudeness, disobedience, or meanness will not give people the idea that you love God. This week, ask God to help you make sure your life has the right fruit in it.

July 9—Matthew 7:16-20
What do you think it means to bear good fruit?

....

July 10—Galatians 5:22-26
I need more of these kinds of fruit in my life:

....

July 11—Psalm 1:1-3
What kind of person does God bless? How can you please Him with your life?

....

July 12—John 15:1-4
What do you have to do to bear good fruit?

....

....

July 13—John 15:5-8

I want to remain in Christ because . . .

July 14—1 Corinthians 13:4-7

If you replaced the word love in these verses with your name, how much of what they say would be true?

July 15—Philippians 1:9-11

Dear God, please help me have more love in my life so that . . .

The Humble Branch

There is an old saying that goes something like this: "The branch with the most fruit bends the lowest." In other words, if a tree branch has more fruit on it than all the other branches, the heavy weight will make it bend toward the ground. When the fruit of the Spirit grows in your life, it should make you humble. That means that you don't think of yourself as better than others . . . just like the heavy tree branch doesn't try to be higher than the others.

What a Character!

Top Traits

Last week we talked about the fruit that others should see in our lives if we call ourselves Christians. This week we're going to look at some other character traits that Christians should have.

Can you figure out these ten words? A few letters have been filled in to get you started. When you finish, write the boxed letters on the lines below to see what Ephesians 5:8 says we should be like. (Don't look up the verse until you're done and want to check your answer!)

Clue	Answer
Concerned about others	☐ _ R _ _ _ G
Not proud	☐ _ M B ☐ _
Does what she's told	_ B _ ☐ _ _ N _
Clean and right	_ U ☐ _
Polite and thoughtful	_ ☐ S P _ C _ F _ _ _
Not greedy	G _ ☐ R _ _ S
Willing to do chores	H _ _ P ☐ _ L
Grateful	_ H _ _ K _ _ ☐
Doesn't hold a grudge	_ _ R G ☐ _ _ N _
Tells the truth	☐ O _ _ _ _ T
Dependable	T _ _ _ T _ O _ ☐ Y

_ _ I _ _ _ _ _ _ / O _ / _ _ G _ _

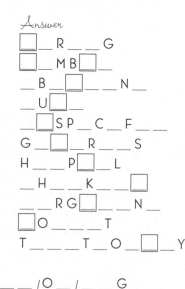

Sticky Situations

You're picking on your little sister and she starts screaming. Your mom pokes her head into the room and tells you to apologize. What do you do? Roll your eyes and mumble, "So-o-o-o-o-r-ry"? Or do you whine that you were just joking?

Having a Christian character means apologizing in a *sincere* way—really feeling in your heart the words that you're saying. Next time turn to your sister and kindly tell her you're sorry you annoyed her. (And then ask God to help you stop bugging her!)

Take a look at these next three situations. Write down how you could show Christian character through the way you respond.

Situation #1: You go to pick up milk at the grocery store and the cashier gives you an extra dollar in change. What do you do?

Situation #2: You lend your best friend your new pink purse for the weekend. On Monday, the zipper's broken. What do you do?

Situation #3: You're watching your favorite TV show when your mom asks you to help her with the laundry. What do you do?

On the next page, draw a comic strip about one of these situations.

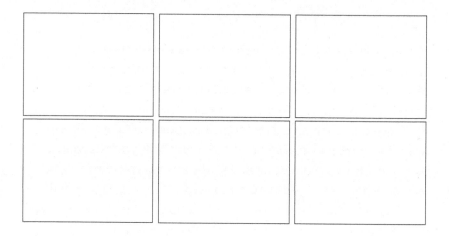

$\mathcal{O}ur$ society puts a lot of emphasis on the *outside* of a person: how much you weigh, what clothes you wear, how you do your hair, what kind of music you listen to, and who you hang out with. If you spend most of your time trying to look good and act cool, what happens to your *inside*—your character? God wants you to focus more on developing a Christian character and becoming the girl He designed you to be. These verses will give you a good start.

July 16—Ephesians 5:3, 15

What are some character traits a Christian *shouldn't* have?

....

....

July 17—Philippians 2:3-4

What do these verses tell you about having Christian character in your relationships?

July 18—Philippians 2:14-15

Dear God, please forgive me for the times I complain and argue. Please help me to . . .

July 19—1 Corinthians 15:33

How do the people you hang around with influence your character?

July 20—Romans 12:9-13

From what you learn in these verses, write two ways you will show Christian character this weekend:

July 21—Romans 12:14-18

When I have difficulties in relationships I can . . .

July 22—2 Peter 1:5-9

Which of the character traits listed in these verses do you need help with?

....

....

God Sees You!

J. C. Watts, a former congressman, youth pastor, and athlete, once said, "Character is doing what's right when nobody's looking."

If you only act like a Christian at church or around your parents, that's called being a hypocrite! Make sure you live the way God wants you to even when you're alone. Remember: You can't hide anything from God!

Dangerous Stuff
The Camel and the Tent

A man sat in his tent on a cold night in the desert. Suddenly, his camel poked his nose in and said, "Master, it's so cold outside! Please let me put my head and neck inside the tent!" The master felt sorry for the camel, so he let him.

The camel moved around for a while and then said, "You know, there's still enough room for me to put my front legs in." The master thought about it and then moved over so the camel could put his legs in.

A little while later the camel said, "I'm keeping the flap of the tent open this way. Maybe I should just come in all the way." The master agreed, so the camel moved all the way in . . . but there was not enough room for both of them!

"Since you're smaller than I am, I think you should stay outside," the camel said, and then he pushed his master out!

This old fable gives a good picture of how temptations seem harmless at first. You may think that it's okay to sin just a little bit once in a while or that some sins are not so bad. The Bible warns that if you don't say no to temptation and sin, they can start to control you!

Watch Out!

Many people do things without realizing that God warns against them because they are spiritually dangerous. What you may think is an innocent game or a harmless activity may confuse your mind and heart and put you on a path that leads away from God and His love and protection.

Dangerous Activities	What's Wrong with Them?	Try These Instead . . .
Checking your horoscope or going to a fortune-teller	You depend on stars and people who may speak with evil spirits to learn about your future.	Ask God to guide you in your choices about the future. You can also get advice from mature Christians you trust.
Doing meditation in yoga and some martial arts or getting hypnotized	You give up control of your mind, which opens the door for the devil and his spirits.	Read your Bible and then spend some time quietly thinking about what you just learned.
Playing with Ouija boards or saying magic spells	You welcome the influence of spiritual powers that are not from God.	Choose activities that don't force you to put your trust in something (or someone) unknown.
Practicing Wicca or witchcraft	You communicate with spirits, and since God forbids this, you can be sure they are evil spirits and not good ones!	Talk to God throughout your day. Surround yourself with godly influences that will keep your mind and heart pure (and safe!).

 164

Talk to your parents, pastor, youth leader, or Sunday school teacher if you need help understanding more about the dangers of these types of activities.

EXTRA CHALLENGE: Write down some specific ways you will avoid harmful spiritual influences. If there are things you watch or activities you participate in that you realize honor evil practices instead of God, ask Him to help you make better choices.

If someone told you to rob a bank or kill your mother, you probably wouldn't have any difficulty saying no! But you *might* be tempted to steal from your friend or be rude to your mother, right? The devil is smart enough to tempt us with sins that don't seem so bad. Once he has hooked us, he starts to tempt us with more and more serious sins. Ask God to give you wisdom and protection!

July 23—1 Peter 5:8-9

How do you think you can be self-controlled and alert against the devil's attacks?

......

......

July 24—James 4:7

What can you do when you feel tempted?

......

......

July 25—1 Thessalonians 5:21-22

Dear God, please help me to stay away from these things:

......

......

July 26—Deuteronomy 18:9-13

What warnings does the Bible give about things like witchcraft?

......

......

......

July 27—2 Corinthians 11:14

I need God's help in recognizing temptation and sin because . . .

July 28—Mark 14:38

How can we protect ourselves from temptation?

July 29—Ephesians 6:10-18

What tools can you use in fighting against temptation and sin?

Not a Cartoon Character!

Forget the little red guy with the horns, goatee, and pitchfork. The devil's not a silly little character that you can just flick off your shoulder. He's a real spirit, he's powerful, and he does everything he can to keep you and me away from God. He doesn't want you to go to heaven, to love God, to live a pure life, or even to have any joy and peace. If you give in to his temptations and live a life full of sin without receiving God's forgiveness, the Bible warns that you will go to hell . . . which is also real!

The awesome thing is that God is *much* more powerful than Satan (the devil) and He can save you from sin and hell. If you haven't yet, put your trust in Jesus today and ask God to help you keep sin out of your life.

Holy Isn't a Swear Word!

Don't Let Your Boat Sink!

Sometimes it may seem impossible to live a pure and perfect Christian life. After all, unless you live in a cabin on a deserted island (and even there it's possible to sin!), you have many negative influences and temptations around you. You live in a world full of other sinful and imperfect people.

Imagine a little rowboat in the middle of a lake. It's in the water and can keep floating on top of it . . . as long as water doesn't get in! Even with a little hole, water will slowly leak into the boat. Once the boat is full of water, it will sink! Someone has to empty out the water and repair the leak.

As a Christian, you live in a world that's surrounded by sin. But you don't have to let the world and its influences into your life. Whenever you're tempted or you sin, ask for God's protection and forgiveness. He can help you remain holy!

Nobody's Perfect!

When you do something wrong, do you make excuses or blame someone else? Do you say, "Well, nobody's perfect"? Of course nobody's perfect . . . but that doesn't mean it's okay to sin.

Let's look at the difference between perfection and holiness. (A lot of people mix those words up!) *Perfection* means making no mistakes and always being completely right. If you were perfect, you would never misunderstand people, you would always know what to do in difficult situations, and you would succeed in everything you did. Jesus was (and is) perfect, and you should try to be like Him as much as possible. But what God wants even more from you is for you to be holy.

Holiness is being "set apart." That means that as a Christian, you need to talk, behave, and live differently from the rest of the world. That means that every day you make it your goal to obey God in every part of your life and not to sin. That might sound impossible—but remember that God never asks you to do anything He won't help you do!

Plan It

In the space below, write some ways you can become holy. Some ideas are listed here to get you started. If you get stuck, try asking your parents, your pastor, or other Christians for their ideas on how to keep yourself holy.

Read my Bible more.

Don't watch shows and movies with bad language, sex, or violence.

Ask God to show me sins I may not realize I'm doing.

Tell my friend I don't want to listen to or spread gossip anymore.

When God designed and created you in His image, His plan included your holiness. When you were born, you "inherited" the spiritual disease of sin—but God has the cure! Believing in His death on the cross, confessing and turning from your sins, and living for Jesus makes you holy. As you'll learn this week, holiness comes only from having a right relationship with God and remaining faithful to Him.

July 30—1 Peter 1:13-16

Why does God expect you to be holy? What are some ways you can do that?

July 31—Hebrews 12:14

What warning does this verse give?

August 1—1 Thessalonians 5:23-24

Dear God, thank You that I don't have to try to be holy by myself and that You . . .

August 2—2 Peter 3:10-11

To live a holy and godly life, how would you need to change?

August 3—2 Corinthians 6:14–7:1

As God's daughter, I need to . . .

August 4—Titus 2:11-14

What does the grace of God teach you?

August 5—Romans 6:19-23

Why is it better to be a slave to righteousness instead of to sin?

The World . . . or God?

James 4:4 warns about being friends with the world. Does that mean God doesn't want you to have friends or to be nice to non-Christians? Nope! This verse teaches that following God should come first in our lives—before entertainment, before shopping, before hanging out with friends, before playing. If other things get more of your attention than God does, can you really say that you love Him? Make your relationship with God your first priority . . . and He will take care of the rest!

Section 5

THE THINGS YOU DO

Your designer genes come with
talents, an imagination, and abilities
that make you uniquely you.
Ready to have fun with them?

The Joy of Journaling
Looking Backward, Looking Forward

Journals are a great way to record meaningful memories or to keep track of your goals. Which of these types of journals would you enjoy keeping? You may decide to have more than one journal!

Diary—Each day (or once in a while) you write down things that happened that you want to remember, or you express how you're feeling about certain things.

Prayer Journal—You write out your prayers to God, telling Him about your day, confessing your sins, asking Him for things you need, and praying for others. Or you can just make a list of things and people you want to pray for each day.

Thankfulness Journal—You write down everything you can think of that you're thankful for or happy about!

Devotional Journal—Every time you read your Bible, you write down what verses you read and what you learned. You may even write down a specific way you will apply that lesson in your life.

Theme Journals—If you're really into sports, music, or world events, you can create a scrapbook where you keep track of interesting facts you learn about that subject.

There are so many types of journals! You can keep a journal where you list all the places you've traveled to, all the restaurants you've eaten at, or all the books you've read. Another idea is to write something interesting about every new person you meet.

Whatever you decide to do, have fun with it . . . and don't forget to flip through your journal once in a while to enjoy the memories you've recorded!

Don't Like Writing?

Not everyone enjoys writing—and that's okay! There are many other neat ways you can journal.

 If you enjoy photography, keep an album or scrapbook of photos that remind you of special events, places, or people.

 Decorate a box or a scrapbook where you keep important souvenirs, such as train tickets, concert programs, encouraging cards and letters, flower petals from someone's wedding or funeral, or even napkins (clean ones!) from cool restaurants.

 If you like drawing or doodling, get a nice sketchbook or unlined notebook and, throughout the day or week, add designs or drawings that help you remember special moments.

What other ideas would fit with your talents and interests?

Tip: Don't forget to write the date at the top of each new page or entry!

Share a Journal

Here's something fun to do with your best friend—or even a group of friends! (You can try this with your family, too.) Get a journal with lots of space to write, draw, or glue things. Write down some thoughts about your friendship or some funny memories. You can draw pictures, add photos or stickers, write jokes, or include anything else you think your friend will enjoy. Take turns writing in the journal, and then pass it back and forth each time you see each other (or if your friend lives far away, through the mail).

You don't have to journal—many people don't! Even if you decide it's not something you would enjoy doing, it's always a good idea to be thankful for the good things that happen in our lives. These blessings come from God! So even if the only journal you have is in your head, try to take time each day to thank God for every good thing (or person!) He sends your way.

August 6—1 Chronicles 16:7-12

What journaling ideas can you get from what David wrote?

August 7—Ecclesiastes 12:1

Why should you make a habit of remembering God's blessings while you're still young?

August 8—Proverbs 3:1-4

Even if you don't keep a journal, why is it important to remember the good things you've been taught?

August 9—Psalm 56:8

Knowing that God keeps a "journal" about me makes me feel . . .

August 10—Hebrews 6:10

God cares enough to remember the good things you do. What are some things you can make a point of remembering?

August 11—Psalm 77:11-13

Dear God, I remember and am thankful for . . .

August 12—Ecclesiastes 7:10, 14

What should you not do when you remember good times in the past?

Watch What You Write!

If you're keeping a private journal where you write down your personal thoughts and feelings, make sure you keep your journal in a private and safe place. Remember: One day someone may find your journal and read it, so try not to write mean or hurtful things about others, or things that would make you feel ashamed.

You Can Do It!

Different People, Different Gifts

You may be surprised to discover how talented some of the people around you are—including yourself! Write down the names of people you think fit into these categories.

Talent	Names
People Smart: Makes friends easily and gets along well with people	
Word Smart: Writes, reads, or communicates well	
Number Smart: Is good at figuring out number or math problems	
Picture Smart: Draws well or is artistic in other ways	
Body Smart: Is athletic or understands a lot about health and fitness	
Music Smart: Sings or plays an instrument well	
Nature Smart: Knows a lot about animals or the environment	

Hidden Talents

How many words with three or more letters can you find using the letters in the word *talents*? You can't use a letter more than the number of times it appears in the original word, and no plural words are allowed (for example, ants). There are at least eleven common three-letter words, nineteen four-letter words, six five-letter words, and two six-letter words. Can you do better?

TALENTS

Check out what these talented people have said about talents:

"A winner is someone who recognizes his God-given talents, works his tail off to develop them into skills, and uses these skills to accomplish his goals."
Larry Bird (basketball star)

"When I stand before God at the end of my life, I would hope that I would not have a single bit of talent left and could say, 'I used everything you gave me.'"
Erma Bombeck (author)

"Talent without discipline is like an octopus on roller skates. There's plenty of movement, but you never know if it's going to be forward, backwards, or sideways."
H. Jackson Brown Jr. (author)

"Talent is God given. Be humble. Fame is man given. Be grateful. Conceit is self-given. Be careful."
John Wooden (basketball coach)

"I tell you, the more I think, the more I feel that there is nothing more truly artistic than to love people."
Vincent Van Gogh (painter)

Once upon a Time . . .

Here's a great story for you to read this week. In Matthew 25:14-30 you'll find one of Jesus' parables (stories He often told His followers to help them understand spiritual lessons). When this parable talks about "talents," it actually means a kind of money. But we should use our money *and* our talents—the things we're good at doing—to please God.

After reading the story, find a way to use one of *your* talents to share this story with someone else. For example, you could act it out, draw a cartoon about it, write the story in your own words, or make up a song about it.

Pray and ask God to show you the talents He has given you . . . and how to use them to bless others!

Everyone

Everyone has talents. Some people have obvious talents, such as singing well, running fast, or being good at math problems. Others have "hidden" talents that are discovered only when people get to know them better. Just remember that your talents come from God and that He wants you to do your best with them. He gave them to you not just so you could think about them or be proud of them but so you can use them to help others and to honor Him.

August 13—Ecclesiastes 9:10

How much effort should you put into using your talents?

August 14—1 Peter 4:9-10

What does God want you to do with your gifts (talents)?

August 15—1 Corinthians 4:1-2, 7

Who do your talents come from? Why shouldn't you brag about your talents?

August 16—Luke 12:48

What does God expect from those who have many talents?

August 17—Isaiah 5:21

Dear God, when I feel too proud about my talents, please help me to . . .

 184

August 18—Jeremiah 18:3-6

Who decides what talents you will have? How are you like a piece of clay in God's hands?

....

....

August 19—Romans 12:4-8

I should use my talents with a humble attitude because . . .

....

....

Look Inside

In the space below, list as many talents as you can think of. Here are some ideas to start you off—including some things you may not have thought of as talents!

encouraging   getting along with people
listening   cooking
organizing   teaching

....

....

....

....

Circle the talents you think you have, and thank God for blessing you with them!

Your Wild Imagination

You Are Creative!

You don't have to enjoy painting or writing to be creative. Even if you don't like art or music, you can still express your own creativity!

Creativity can mean coming up with new and interesting ways to do old things, or taking something old and making it look new and fresh. Creativity can mean solving difficult problems or puzzles by thinking about things in a different way. It can mean making up fun games or inventing things.

If you don't think you're very creative, don't worry about it! Some people are more creative than others, but all of us have *some* creative abilities. We'll look more closely at this in our Bible readings this week. If you think of yourself as a creative person, ask God to show you how you can use that ability to honor Him.

Remember: Creativity doesn't mean coming up with something brilliant or perfect every time. It means using your imagination, trying different things, and having fun while you do it.

Try Something New

This week, pick at least one of these activities and give your creative muscles some exercise. The results may surprise you!

❋ Make up a secret language just for you and your best friend.

❋ Think of ten unusual things you can do with a spoon. (Believe it or not, there's one girl who turned a long spoon into a bracelet!)

✳ Write a story using just the words you cut out from one page in a magazine or newspaper.

✳ Think of a fun theme for someone's birthday party.

✳ Make yourself a sandwich that's completely different from anything you've had before, or make a meal using foods that are all the same color.

✳ Come up with a list of things your family can do during a power failure.

✳ Make up a word puzzle.

✳ Think of your own ideas for creative activities!

The Greatest Creator

In the space below, write down all the things you can think of that God created. Some examples have been given to get you started. When you finish your list, circle the things you find amazingly creative. Take a moment to thank God for them!

peacocks
rainbows
waterfalls

babies
diamonds
fingerprints

The Bible tells us that God created all the wonderful things in this world. We know that He also created people in His image. That means that He made you with the ability to imagine and create and design too! Of course, you don't have the same wisdom and power that God does, but you can thank Him for the creativity He has given you and use it to please Him.

August 20—Isaiah 40:26

How do you feel when you read about the care God used to create the universe?

August 21—Ephesians 4:22-24

I believe that God created me to . . .

August 22—Deuteronomy 8:17-18

Why should you be humble about your creativeness?

August 23—Psalm 127:1

Why should you ask God for help with your ideas and the projects you work on?

....

August 24—Psalm 19:1-3

What reminds you about God's awesome creativity?

....

August 25—Hebrews 3:3

Just as you are more important than the things you create, invent, or make, what should your attitude be toward God who created you?

....

August 26—Jeremiah 10:14-15

Dear God, please help me not to value the things I create too much because . . .

....

Use It Wisely!

Sometimes people use their abilities for selfish and wrong reasons. As we've seen during the last two weeks, God has blessed us with talents and creativity, but He expects us to use them in ways that help people and honor Him. With God's help, stay away from ways that creativity can go wrong, such as:

❋ thinking and acting like you are more special than others

❋ planning ways to embarrass or be mean to someone

❋ tricking people into believing things that aren't true

❋ exaggerating the truth to get people to like you

Good Medicine

Proverbs 17:22 says that "a cheerful heart is good medicine." These jokes from Emily, Kristen, and Emma—girls your age in Ontario, Canada—are for your funny bone!

QUESTION: What do you get when Batman and Robin are run over by a steamroller?
ANSWER: Flatman and Ribbon!
—Emily

Knock, knock.
Who's there?
Amos.
Amos who?
A mosquito just bit you! Ha-ha!
—Kristen

QUESTION: What did the karate instructor say to the new student?
ANSWER: Hi-ya!
—Emma

Grown-Up Hopscotch

Do you think hopscotch is too babyish? Try this instead!

1. Find a sidewalk or a large driveway where you can draw with chalk.

2. Make a "board game" by drawing a row of at least ten squares (make each square big enough to stand inside with both feet). The line of squares can go straight, in a circle, or in a winding path—whatever design you want, as long as it's easy to get from one square to the next.

3. Just before the first square, write the word *START.* That's where all the players will stand before they play their first turn. In the last square, write the word *FINISH.*

4. Write instructions in at least five of the squares. Some examples: "Sing a song," "Go back 3 spaces," "Jump 10 times," "Tell a joke," or "Advance 1 space."

5. Draw a circle (about the size of a dinner plate) near the squares and divide it into six even spaces. Write the numbers 1 to 6 in the spaces.

6. Get a small stone for each player. Take turns throwing them on the numbers and advancing by the number the stone landed on. If a player lands on a square with instructions, she must do what it says.

7. The first player to reach *FINISH* wins!

Road Trip

Does your family spend a lot of time in the car, driving from place to place? Here's a fun game that will give your brain some exercise. Agree on a category (or choose a few categories ahead of time). Then take turns going through the alphabet, with each player naming one thing that fits into the category. For example, if you choose girls' names as a category, the answers could be Amy, Beth, Christina, Danielle, Esther, and so on.

Here are some other categories you can use: names of places, types of food, boys' names, types of clothing, and book titles.

Write your own category ideas here:

_____   _____

_____   _____

_____   _____

_____

We've talked about a lot of serious subjects so far in *Designer Genes*. But this week we're talking about fun and laughter. Although God doesn't want you to spend all your time just doing things that are fun for yourself, it's okay to take a break sometimes, laugh a little, have a good time with friends and family, and enjoy the blessings God has given you. That's why we have things like breaks at school, weekends, and holidays!

August 27—Proverbs 15:30

What does this verse say about having a cheerful, positive attitude?

August 28—Psalm 126:1-3

Dear God, I have joy in my heart because . . .

August 29—Ecclesiastes 2:1-2, 10-11

Why should you be careful about focusing too much on having fun?

August 30—Ecclesiastes 3:1, 4

I need to remember that . . .

August 31—Proverbs 15:13

What are some ways you can keep your heart truly happy?

September 1—Exodus 23:12

Why do you think God wants us to take one day in the week to rest?

September 2—Job 8:20-21

How can you still have hope and joy, even when you don't feel happy or when life gets tough?

Fun . . . and Free!

The next time you and your friends feel bored, why not skip the TV and the computer? Instead, have a blast with games from your past! Remember how fun some of the kids' games you used to play were? Try some of these fun outdoor and indoor games again. Bonus: They don't cost anything!

Duck, Duck, Goose
Marco Polo (in the pool!)
Hide-and-Seek
Tag
Hot Potato

Broken Telephone
Simon Says
Charades
Rock, Paper, Scissors

Note: If you're not sure how to play these games, ask an adult or see if you can look them up in a game book or on the Internet.

Write down your own ideas for fun and free games:

 196

Take Care!

Ready, Set . . . Babysit!

How do you know when you're ready to become a babysitter?
There isn't an exact age that suddenly makes you mature enough,
although you may want to wait until you're closer to high school.
If you've got the desire, though, that's a good start! Why not ask
your parents what they think? (You need their permission first
anyway, of course.)

HERE ARE SOME QUESTIONS TO ASK YOURSELF:

 Do I like babies and children? If little kids get on your
nerves, then you probably wouldn't make a very good
babysitter!

 Do I enjoy taking care of people? Babysitting isn't just
about playing with younger children—or about earning
extra money. It's about understanding what they need,
caring about them, and helping them.

 Do I know what to do? If you're going to take care of
babies, you have to know how to do things like change
their diapers and feed them.

 Am I dependable? If you cancel appointments a lot or show
up late, that's not a good way to develop someone else's
trust. You must also respect the rules set by the parents.

Am I alert? When there's a problem, you have to be able to think quickly and come up with a solution.

Am I creative? When you're looking after young children, you often have to think of lots of fun activities and games to keep them busy.

If you're not quite ready to babysit yet, don't worry! You can start preparing yourself by taking babysitting and first aid courses (try your community center or the Red Cross). Volunteer to help take care of your younger siblings or cousins sometimes, or help out in your church's nursery. Taking care of pets is another way to learn responsibility. You can also offer to babysit at your own home, with your parents around to watch and help you as you learn.

Who Cares?

Using the code below, fill in the letters for each word and you'll discover a great reminder about caring for others (from Philippians 2:4).

A = 1	H = 8	O = 15	V = 22
B = 2	I = 9	P = 16	W = 23
C = 3	J = 10	Q = 17	X = 24
D = 4	K = 11	R = 18	Y = 25
E = 5	L = 12	S = 19	Z = 26
F = 6	M = 13	T = 20	
G = 7	N = 14	U = 21	

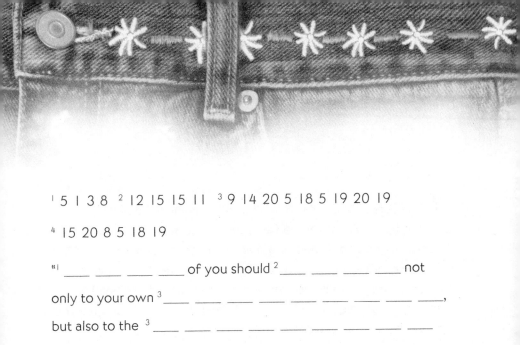

¹ 5 1 3 8 ² 12 15 15 11 ³ 9 14 20 5 18 5 19 20 19

⁴ 15 20 8 5 18 19

"¹ ____ ____ ____ ____ of you should ² ____ ____ ____ ____ not

only to your own ³____ ____ ____ ____ ____ ____ ____ ____ ____,

but also to the ³ ____ ____ ____ ____ ____ ____ ____ ____ ____

of ⁴ ____ ____ ____ ____ ____ ____."

Bible 9-1-1

Part of the responsibility of taking care of someone or babysitting is knowing what to do in an emergency. You probably learned at a very young age to dial 9-1-1 during an emergency, such as a fire or an accident. Here are some great "9:11" Bible verses to encourage you.

> Genesis 9:11—a promise that God made to the world
>
> Psalm 9:11—a reminder to praise God
>
> Proverbs 9:11—another promise from God, if we trust in Him
>
> Ecclesiastes 9:11—a reminder that we are all equal
>
> Luke 9:11—a description of how Jesus took care of people

SOLUTION: "Each of you should look not only to your own interests, but also to the interests of others."

These years of your life are a mixture of being a kid but also growing up. You're at the perfect age to start learning to take on responsibilities and developing skills you will need later in life. This week, why not ask God to give you opportunities to try taking care of others? It could be babysitting small children or helping someone of any age who is hurt and needs help. God can give you a caring heart—just like Jesus'!

September 3—1 Thessalonians 2:7-8

How can you show others, especially children, that you love them?

....
....

September 4—Isaiah 40:11

What can you learn from God's example?

....
....

September 5—Luke 18:15-17

How do you feel about the way Jesus treated children?

....
....

September 6—2 Timothy 2:24

My attitude toward others should be . . .

....
....

 200

September 7—Mark 9:42

What warning does the Bible give about being a bad example to small children?

September 8—James 1:27

Dear God, please help me to . . .

September 9—2 Timothy 4:5

How should you react when you face difficulties while taking care of someone?

Be a CSI!

If you want to start learning about taking care of babies and toddlers . . . become a Child-Sitting Investigator! Ask some mothers you know, perhaps at your church or in your neighborhood, what qualities they expect in a babysitter. If you hear anything you hadn't thought of before, write it down here as a reminder:

Flower Power

Weed This!

Weeds are plants that you don't want growing in your garden
. . . but they show up anyway! No matter how hard you work to
have beautiful flowers, if you don't pull out those weeds, they
will choke out the rest of your plants and make your garden look
ugly. And if you don't pull them out right away, they'll grow bigger
and stronger and it will become harder to get rid of them later.

Our hearts are like gardens. It's not enough for us to love good
things. We also have to hate sin! If we don't ask God every day to
forgive us and to help us not to disobey Him, those sins become
sticky bad habits in our lives, just like weeds.

Next time you realize you've sinned, ask God right away to
pull out that weed. Keep doing that, and your life will become as
beautiful as a garden!

Where Do You Start?

If you live in an apartment building or have never helped someone
in a garden, you may not know much about gardening. No problem!

Ask your parents if you can get a small flowering plant in a pot
to take care of. Follow the instructions carefully (how much light
it needs, how much to water it) and see what happens. If your
plant does well, you can try getting other plants.

If your parents, grandparents, or neighbors have gardens, ask if you can watch them while they work. They can teach you about different plants, and maybe you'll even get to help out!

Crazy Daisies and Silly Lilies!

How well do you know your flowers? Look up these flowers in an encyclopedia or on the Internet and draw a picture of each one.

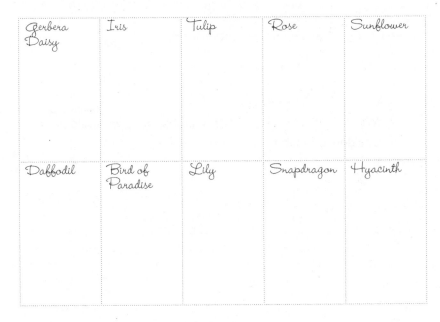

Gerbera Daisy	Iris	Tulip	Rose	Sunflower
Daffodil	Bird of Paradise	Lily	Snapdragon	Hyacinth

Which flower do you like the most? Color it in!

In many places, the Bible compares our relationships with God to a gardener and his plants. A good gardener knows how to take care of his plants so that they'll grow up to become strong, healthy trees or flowers. Just as a plant needs sunlight, water, and good soil, we need to spend time with God, our Gardener, and dig into His Word, the Bible.

September 10—Isaiah 58:11
I can trust in God because He promises to . . .

....

....

September 11—Jeremiah 17:7-8
What do you think verse 8 means? What happens when you put your confidence in God?

....

....

September 12—Psalm 103:15-18
What is one way we are different from God?

....

....

September 13—Psalm 92:12-15

What kinds of people become beautiful and healthy "plants" in God's garden?

....

....

September 14—Proverbs 11:18-21

Sowing means planting. What should you plant if you want to receive God's blessings?

....

....

September 15—Luke 8:4-15

Which of these four seeds reminds you of yourself? Why?

....

....

September 16—Galatians 6:7-10

Dear God, please help me to . . .

....

....

....

Taking Care of Cut Flowers

Have you ever put beautiful flowers in a vase and then found them dead a couple of days later? Here are some tips to make them last longer:

 Always start with a clean vase and fill it about halfway with fresh water.

 If the flowers are too tall, cut the stems under running water and then put them in the vase right away.

 Take off any leaves that are under the water.

 Don't put the vase where there's too much sunlight or on your television. If the flowers get too warm, they grow faster and die sooner.

 Change the water every two days.

Let's Play House

Helpful Hands Quiz

Circle the answers that are closest to what you would do.

1. **When your mom tells you to clean your room, you . . .**
   a) shove all your stuff under your bed and into drawers and hope she won't check.
   b) hang up your clothes, straighten up your desk, and put away the big stuff.
   c) put everything back in its place, dust your furniture, sweep or vacuum your floor, and empty your trash can.

2. **When your favorite skirt gets a hole in it, you . . .**
   a) throw it out and buy a new one.
   b) ask your mom to mend it for you.
   c) get a patch and thread and mend it yourself.

3. **When your family finishes eating dinner, you . . .**
   a) go back to doing your own thing.
   b) put your dishes in the sink and help clear the table.
   c) wash the dishes, dry them, and put them away.

4. When your mom is sick in bed . . .

    a) your dad or another adult has to prepare meals and clean the house.

    b) you make peanut butter and jelly sandwiches for everyone.

    c) you take care of her and also do the laundry, cooking, and cleaning.

If you answered mostly A, you need to work on your lazy attitude! Ask God to help you be more helpful around the house.

If you answered mostly B, you probably understand the importance of doing chores. But you can always do better!

If you answered mostly C, you're a domestic diva! Keep up the good work!

Make a Job Jar

If you want to help out more at home but don't know where to start, try this. Write the following chores on slips of paper and put them all in a jar. (You can add your own ideas too!) Pull a job out of the jar every day or every week and ask your parents how you can help with that chore. You'll make them happy . . . and you'll learn some important skills that you will need when you're older.

Changing bedsheets
Cleaning bathrooms
Cleaning the fridge
Cooking
Dusting
Doing laundry
Doing yard work

Setting the table
Sweeping
Taking out the recycling
Taking out the trash
Vacuuming
Washing dishes
Washing the car

Growing up isn't just about having more freedom. It's also about having more responsibilities. When you think about everything your parents have done for you, doesn't it make you want to help them out with some of the work at home? God wants you to honor your parents by pitching in. He also wants you to become the best you can be—and that includes learning to take care of a home.

September 17—Romans 12:13

How can learning to do things around the house help you be a blessing to other people?

September 18—1 Peter 4:9-10

What do these verses tell you about the attitude you should have when serving others?

September 19—2 Thessalonians 3:11-13

How does God want you to spend your free time?

....

....

September 20—Proverbs 14:1

Dear God, I ask You to give me wisdom because . . .

....

....

September 21—Titus 2:4-5

What does God expect from young women? Are there parts of this passage that apply to you now?

....

....

September 22—Proverbs 31:10-17

What qualities does a good wife have? What can you learn from these verses?

....

....

September 23—Luke 10:38-42

What is even more important than being good at housework?

....

....

Ant Lessons

Proverbs 6:6-8 tells us to be like ants! If you've ever watched a bunch of ants on the sidewalk or in a field, you've probably seen how hard they work. Who tells them to do their chores? No one! They just know that if they don't collect food and store it up for winter, they will starve and die. They have enough wisdom to work hard now and rest later. How can you be more like an ant?

Manners Matter!

Do You Have Good Etiquette?

"Manners are a sensitive awareness of the feelings of others. If you have that awareness, you have good manners, no matter what fork you use."

Emily Post

Emily Post became famous after writing a book about etiquette (good manners) in 1922, and people still follow her advice today. If you feel like you can't remember all the rules of etiquette, just remember Ms. Post's advice above. As long as you stop to think about how your actions or words will make someone else feel, you will probably show good manners. Ask God to help you care about the feelings of others and to be as kind and gentle as you can.

Mixed-Up Utensils!

Part of etiquette is having some of the homekeeping skills we talked about last week. Do you know which of the following pictures shows a correct arrangement for how to set a table?

1.

2.

3.

4.

Here's an easy tip from the Emily Post Institute to help you remember proper place settings. Think of the word *FORKS* (but forget about the letter R). From left to right, place the fork (letter F), plate (shape of an O), knife (letter K), and spoon (letter S).

SOLUTION: Number 2 is correct. It would also be okay to put the napkin on top of the plate.

Bad Manners Are Never Cool!

How many of these things do you do? Answer honestly!

- ☐ talk with your mouth full
- ☐ put your elbows on the table while eating
- ☐ reach across the table to get something instead of asking someone to pass it
- ☐ slurp loudly while eating soup or drinking
- ☐ stuff your whole mouth with food
- ☐ blow bubbles or make snapping sounds with your gum
- ☐ interrupt people while they're talking
- ☐ yell across the house when you want to tell a family member something
- ☐ forget to say thank you to people
- ☐ talk during church
- ☐ talk during movies
- ☐ put your feet up on the chair in front of you in a theatre
- ☐ don't say hello to your friends' parents on the phone or at their house
- ☐ show up late for activities
- ☐ stay seated when an older person gets on the bus or subway
- ☐ don't hold doors open for people
- ☐ stare at people with physical disabilities

If you checked five or more of these, you need to work on your manners! Test yourself again in a few weeks and see if your etiquette has improved.

When you leave an event or someone's home, how do you think people remember you? No matter what your friends do, remember that bad manners are never cool! No one will respect you if you behave badly or speak rudely. Worse than that, you will give people a bad impression of how a Christian acts and treats others. Remember, as a child of God the King, you should behave like royalty!

September 24—Colossians 4:6
Dear God, in my conversations with others, please help me to . . .

September 25—Leviticus 19:32
How does God want you to treat older people?

September 26—1 Peter 2:17
Who are some people in your life you need to show more respect to?

September 27—Titus 3:1-2
After reading these verses, how do you think you need to improve your manners?

September 28—Luke 17:11-19

Dear God, please help me remember to say thank you! People I need to thank this week:

September 29—Titus 2:11-12

How does the grace of God teach you to behave?

September 30—Proverbs 4:10-13

Why is it wise to listen to good advice?

Let Your Example Shine

Try some of these examples of excellent etiquette and see how many people notice. They may even pick up some of these good habits themselves!

 When you are introduced to a new person, smile, look into her eyes, and say, "I'm happy to meet you!"

 Throw out your trash and put away your tray in fast-food restaurants.

 Say thank you and smile at whoever serves you in a store or a restaurant.

 Sit properly in public. That means no slouching in your chair and keeping both feet on the floor in front of you.

 Don't barge into other people's rooms. Knock first and wait to be invited in.

Wonderful Words

Palindromes

A palindrome is a word or phrase that reads the same backward or forward. Here are some examples:

> Race car
> Lonely Tylenol
> Yo, banana boy!
> Straw warts
> We panic in a pew!
> Was it a cat I saw?

Try making up some of your own!

Comment ça va?

Want to learn some common phrases in a foreign language to wow your friends? (Hey, *wow* is another palindrome!) Here's how you ask, "How are you?" (informally) in several different languages:

Greek: *Ti kaneis?*

Tagalog: *Kumusta ka?*

Bengali: *Kemon acho?*

Spanish: *¿Cómo estás?*

Yiddish: *Vos makhtsu?*

German: *Wie geht's?*

Lithuanian: *Kaip laikaisi?*

Italian: *Come stai?*

Russian: *Kak dela?*

Cantonese: *Nei ho ma?*

Psst! *Comment ça va?* literally means "How's it going?" in French.

Tacky Worms!

Spoonerisms are another way to have fun with language . . . except when they happen by mistake and you get embarrassed! Have you ever mixed up the sounds of the first letters of two words in your sentence, and it actually made sense but in a funny way? For example, "tacky worms" is a spoonerism of "wacky terms."

A few more tacky worms:

I have to shake a tower (take a shower).
My sister has mad banners (bad manners).
Tomorrow we're going to chew some doors (do some chores).
It's roaring pain outside (pouring rain).

Now you sink of thumb!

Fun Fact: Spoonerisms got their name from a minister named Reverend William Archibald Spooner (born in 1844), who used to mix up his words this way quite often when he was speaking.

Our Designer has given us the wonderful gift of words and language, which we use to communicate with people, to express our thoughts, to tell stories, and to learn. Like anything else, though, if we don't use this gift properly—the way God wants us to—we can cause a lot of harm.

October 1—Psalm 34:12-14

My thoughts:

October 2—Ecclesiastes 5:2-7

How good are you at keeping your word when you make a promise? What improvements can you make?

October 3—James 3:3-9

What does this passage teach you about your words?

October 4—Psalm 37:30-31

Dear God, help me to . . .

October 5—Psalm 139:1-4

How do you feel about God knowing your thoughts before you even say them out loud?

October 6—1 Timothy 4:12; 1 Peter 3:9-12

What do these verses teach you?

....

....

October 7—Ephesians 4:29; James 4:11-12

How do you think God wants you to change the way you speak about others?

....

....

Vitalize Your Vocabulary!

When reading difficult books or studying the Bible, keep a small notebook and a dictionary handy. Look up and write down the definitions of new words to build up your vocabulary. Try writing or saying your own sentences using the words you discover. You can ask a parent or a teacher to check them for you. If you keep doing this, you'll soon be *voluble* and *verbose*!

Section 6

THE WORLD AROUND YOU

How does your Designer expect you to interact with other cultures, people in need, nature, and animals? He designed those, too!

What's Going On?

It's a Scary World Out There!

We asked some girls what worried them the most about the things happening around the world. They answered:

 Wars, terrorists, and bombings

People cutting down a lot of trees

People killing animals

Poor people

Global warming and the hole in the ozone layer

People dying of disease and hunger

Cancer

People wasting things

Crime

Pollution

What about you? What issues worry you? Write out a prayer here, telling God about your fears and concerns:

How Can I Cope?

Hearing about wars, natural disasters, or terrible accidents can really make you feel afraid or nervous . . . especially if the situation is close to where you live. You may feel helpless, wondering what you can do to make things better.

God has given you the ability to feel compassion and concern—it's in your "designer genes"—but He has also given you a way to cope with your fears. Better than any best friend you could ever have, God will listen to you at any time of day, for as long as you want to talk with Him. He may seem far away at times, but His Spirit is with you and He knows everything that's happening in the world. Even when things are difficult, you can trust Him. You can ask Him to give you peace in your heart even when you don't see peace in the world, in your school, or in your family.

Puzzle Peace

King David had many things troubling him, but he knew where to go for help. Unscramble the letters on the puzzle pieces to discover how David viewed God. Then read Psalm 32:7 to see what he meant.

Write the letters in order here: __ __ __ __ __ __ / __ __ __ __ __

Problems have always existed in the world—since the time of Creation! Jesus never promised that we would have world peace or that poverty would disappear. He warned His disciples—and us—that we will have troubles. But He also promised to be with us, to help us, and to give us peace in our hearts.

October 8—Philippians 4:6-7
What happens when you bring your concerns to God?

October 9—Matthew 24:6-13
Why should you not feel surprised by what happens in the world? What promise does Jesus give in these verses?

October 10—Psalm 91:14-16
How does God help those who love Him?

October 11—John 14:27; 16:33
Dear God, thank You that . . .

October 12—Isaiah 26:3-4

What can you do to have peace in your life?

....

....

October 13—Isaiah 54:10

Even in the worst situations, why can you still have hope?

....

....

October 14—Romans 8:31-39

These verses encourage me because . . .

....

....

Why Does God Let All This Stuff Happen?

Sometimes people wonder whether God really cares about the bad things that go on in the world. They ask why He doesn't stop them from happening. When God created human beings, He gave us a special characteristic: *free will.* We have the ability to make our own decisions. We can choose between right and wrong. We can choose to obey God or disobey Him. God didn't make us puppets . . . or robots!

Most of the bad things that happen in the world come from choices that people make. God can help you make a difference by shining His light into the world and showing people a better way to live. You can also remind people about all the wonderful blessings God *does* give us, even though we don't deserve them, such as health, food, sunshine, protection, family and friends, jobs, and education.

 226

Send Me!

Willing or Unwilling?

In Isaiah 6, the prophet Isaiah describes a vision, or dream, he had about God. In it, he heard God ask, "Whom shall I send? And who will go for us?" Without hesitating, Isaiah answered: "Here am I. Send me!" God had an important message for the people in Isaiah's country, but He needed someone to deliver that message for Him. Isaiah gladly volunteered!

Not everyone in the Bible was so willing to go on a mission for God, though. Jonah 1:1-3 tells the famous story of how Jonah ran away from God instead of agreeing to go to Nineveh to warn the people there about their wickedness. And in Exodus 3–4, we read about all the excuses Moses made when God asked him to go to Egypt and free the Jewish slaves. In both of these stories we see that God was not pleased with reluctance.

God has blessed you with many talents and gifts, and He has a plan for your life. That plan includes helping others and sharing God's love with them. Will you run away from responsibilities like Jonah and Moses did . . . or will you raise your hand and say, "Here am I! Send me!"

What Can I Do?

Studies show that teenagers volunteer more than any other age group does! Check out these ideas and add some of your own. Then ask your parents or other adults to help you get started.

(If they can't drive you, start with something you can do at home, at church, in your school, or in your neighborhood.)

❋ Play checkers with senior citizens at a nursing home.

❋ Serve soup at a homeless shelter or bake cookies for the homeless.

❋ Clean up the garbage in a city park.

❋ Tutor a younger student in your school.

❋ Help organize your church library.

❋ Read books to children in the hospital.

❋ Write cards to sick people in your church.

❋ Make and sell crafts and send the money to missionaries.

❋ Grow your hair long and give it away for cancer patients' wigs.

Your ideas:

Dizzy Donations

Unscramble the words on the next page to discover some things that others may need and you can give away!

meit	otys
othcsle	sleegseyas
ooskb	segma
meyon	hira
umpocret	fodo
clyeibc	fracts

We live in a selfish world, where most people think only about themselves and complain when they don't have what they want. Does that describe you, too? When you volunteer your time, share your money, or help people in some other way, it gets your mind off yourself and your problems. You realize how much you have to thank God for when you see the difficulties of others. The Bible says a lot about the importance of serving others. Check it out:

October 15—1 John 3:16-18

Why should you, as a Christian, be eager to help others?

_____

_____

October 16—Acts 20:35

Dear God, please give me the desire to . . .

October 17—Luke 14:12-14

What should your motivation (or reasons) be for volunteering?

October 18—Luke 6:38

What does God promise to those who give others their time or money?

October 19—Proverbs 21:13

What warning does this verse give?

October 20—Matthew 25:34-40

I can please God and bless others by . . .

October 21—Matthew 6:1-4

What attitude should you have when you help those in need?

....

....

Wise Words

Helen Keller, born in Alabama in 1880, wasn't even two years old when a terrible sickness made her blind and deaf. Amazingly, with the help of a patient teacher named Anne Sullivan, Helen learned to communicate by making signs on people's palms and touching their lips and throats while they spoke. When she grew up, her books, speeches, and fund-raising efforts helped many people with disabilities.

Helen Keller once said, "The unselfish effort to bring cheer to others will be the beginning of a happier life for ourselves."

How will *you* bring cheer to someone this week?

Around the World in Seven Days

Travel the World . . . without Leaving Home!

If someone blindfolded you and then dropped you in the middle of Los Angeles or Toronto, it might take you a while to figure out what country you were in! In big cities like these, you can see people from all over the world and hear many different languages.

It's wonderful to get to know and learn from different cultures and nationalities. But what if you live in a small town without many immigrants or ethnic groups? How can you grow to appreciate people from other cultures? You can find out about them without even leaving your house! Many interesting Web sites, books, and movies teach about people and customs around the world. Ask your parents if you can get a pen pal or if you can sponsor a poor child in another country. If your church helps any foreign missionaries, ask for information about them and pray for them. Write them encouraging letters—they may even write back and tell you about the people they work with!

That's Not English!

Can you match the twelve words or phrases on the left, which come from different cultures around the world, with their definitions on the right?

A. mosque (Arabic)

B. souvlaki (Greek)

C. à la carte (French)

D. pierogi (Polish)

E. smorgasbord (Swedish)

F. siesta (Spanish)

G. wok (Cantonese)

H. dachshund (German)

I. karaoke (Japanese)

J. fiesta (Spanish)

K. escargot (French)

L. phobia (Greek)

1. a menu where every item is listed separately with its own price

2. a type of frying pan

3. when someone sings along with recorded music

4. a festival or holiday

5. cooked snails

6. a place of worship for followers of Islam

7. an unreasonable fear of something

8. a small pie, usually with meat, potato, or cabbage inside

9. cubes of roasted pork or lamb meat, usually served in pita bread

10. a small dog with a long, shiny body and short legs

11. an afternoon nap

12. a meal where there are a lot of different foods to choose from

233

Babbling at Babel

How many languages do you think there are in the world? 150? 645? 1,300? Would you believe that at least 6,800 languages have been discovered? About 2,260 of these have writing systems (the rest are only spoken languages). How many languages do you know?

Do you know how or why people first started to speak in different languages? Check out the story of the tower of Babel in Genesis 11:1-9. We don't know how many languages those people spoke, but we can see what happened when they became too proud and tried to take the honor that belongs to God.

Modern technology has made it easier for people around the world to meet each other and to learn about other cultures. We can travel quickly by airplane, we have long-distance phones, and then there's the Internet. But we still see a lot of racism—people judging others because of their skin color, language, or cultural background. Let's see what the Bible teaches.

October 22—Galatians 3:28

What attitude should you have toward people who are different from you?

October 23—Acts 10:28

How does God feel about racism?

October 24—Romans 10:12-14

Dear God, please help me not to feel shy about sharing my faith with others because . . .

October 25—Proverbs 18:1-2

What do these verses tell you about being open to different people and their opinions?

October 26—Acts 10:34-35

I can have an attitude that's more like God's if I . . .

October 27—James 2:1, 8-10

How should you treat the people around you?

October 28—Philippians 2:9-11

No matter what culture or country people come from, what will everyone do one day?

Respect . . . or Accept?

You can learn a lot by making friends with people from different cultural backgrounds (and you can try some yummy new foods, too!). You may not always understand the customs of other nationalities, but it's important to show respect, no matter how strange you may find their style of dress, language, or lifestyle.

However, respecting someone's culture does not mean accepting her religion . . . especially if it contradicts the Bible. Ask God to always show you what's true and to help you share your faith with your friends in a courageous but respectful way.

Love Your Neighbor

Next Door . . . and All Around!

You may think of your neighbors as the people who live in the house next door, in the apartment above yours, or on the next farm. That would make it easier to love your neighbor, as Jesus asks us to do, since you'd only have to try to love a few people.

Think again! Your neighbor can be the girl sitting near you in class, the boy whose locker is next to yours, the lady who drives your bus, the old man who works at the grocery store, the high schooler on the bench next to you at the park . . . or anyone walking by you on the street!

Each day, ask God to help you show kindness and love to everyone you meet—not just your next-door neighbors.

Block Party!

Arrange the blocks on the next page in the right order, and you'll see what the Bible teaches in Romans 12:18 about our relationships with others—including our neighbors. To help, we've shown you how many letters each word has. See if you can figure it out before looking up the verse.

| p e a | i t h | e a t | L i v |
| e v e | n e . | r y o | c e w |

Write the answer here:

___ ___ ___ ___ / ___ ___ / ___ ___ ___ ___ ___

___ ___ ___ ___ / ___ ___ ___ ___ ___ ___ ___ ___ ___ .

Good Neighbors

We know that your neighbors are more than just the people who live nearby . . . but those next-door neighbors are important too! Here are some ideas from girls your age about how to be a good neighbor. Check out their suggestions . . . and then write down your own ideas. Whenever you do something on the list, come back and put a smiley face next to it.

* Say hello and be friendly to your neighbors.

* Feed their cats and take in their mail when they're away.

* Help them shovel their driveways.

* Don't gossip about them.

SOLUTION: Live at peace with everyone.

✳ Be polite.

✳ Help them with their yard work.

✳ Invite them over for dinner.

✳ Bake special treats for them.

The commandment to "love your neighbor" appears ten times in the Bible. Obviously, God wants us to remember this important rule. It's not enough to say that we love God. He wants us to show that we truly love Him by treating others with love and honor too. As you read this week's verses, pay close attention to what kind of neighbor you are. If you need to change, tell God about it. He'll help you!

October 29—Leviticus 19:18

How does God want you to treat people when they upset you?

October 30—Proverbs 3:27-29

Dear God, when someone around me has a problem, please help me to . . .

October 31—Luke 10:25-37

What can you learn about being a good neighbor from this story?

November 1—1 Thessalonians 5:14-15

Write the names of some people you need to show more patience and kindness to. Then ask God to help you.

November 2—Deuteronomy 5:21

Dear God, please forgive me for being jealous of . . .

November 3—Psalm 101:5

How does God feel when you gossip or think you're better than someone else?

November 4—Matthew 5:38-48

What kind of attitude does God want you to have, not just toward your neighbors, but also toward your enemies?

_____

_____

Not Number One!

Have you ever noticed that many people think of themselves as "number one"? We have all kinds of competitions and contests to see who's the best at something—soccer, singing, spelling, science, or skating.

It's okay to participate in competitions, but make sure you're not always trying to prove that you're better than others. Remember what you've learned this week: You must love others the way you love yourself!

Only One Earth

Taking Care of God's Creation

In Genesis 1, the Bible describes how God created the earth, animals, and people. If you take a drive through the countryside, hike through the woods, swim in the ocean, or walk around a flower garden, it's easy to see what a wonderful Designer God is! He gave us a beautiful home to live in (Earth), and we're responsible for taking care of it and keeping it clean—just as we should keep our houses or apartments in good condition.

When humans don't care about the earth, that neglect harms nature and the environment. We waste natural resources, such as water, trees, and other good things that the earth produces. We pollute rivers and the air. We make disgusting piles of trash. This week, think about the respect (or disrespect!) that people show God's creation . . . and what you can do about it.

Reuse, Reduce, Recycle

In rich countries, people throw out tons of trash every day! A lot of the things we buy have much more packaging than they need. We also have the bad habit of throwing things out once we've used them or grown tired of them instead of *reusing* them or giving them away. Thankfully, many people do care about the environment and have found cool ways to *reduce* waste. People are also learning that many things can be *recycled*.

It's time to use your imagination and creativity! Some of the following items can be recycled . . . but can you think of ways they might also be reused?

plastic bags
old magazines
empty shampoo bottles
empty CD cases
old CDs
empty cereal boxes
old towels
cardboard tubes
broken jewelry
old birthday cards
empty tissue boxes
shoelaces from old shoes

Throw a Re-Party!

Want to get your friends thinking about the environment? Why not organize a "re-party"?

 Write the invitations on paper or cardboard that you've recycled from other things.

 Ask your friends to bring "junk" they want to reuse or recycle (such as the examples listed above). They can also bring bits of ribbon or string, scrap paper, and any other small items that are clean but seem useless.

 Supply scissors, glue, and tape, but no other new craft supplies.

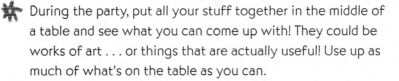 During the party, put all your stuff together in the middle of a table and see what you can come up with! They could be works of art . . . or things that are actually useful! Use up as much of what's on the table as you can.

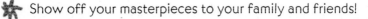 Show off your masterpieces to your family and friends!

God made humans more special than nature and animals—He made us in His image—but that doesn't mean it's okay to treat the earth badly. A lot of the problems in our environment today have been caused by people's selfishness and greediness. Those are not qualities that Christians should have, and no matter how old you are, you can set a good example of honoring God, the great Designer, by honoring the earth He created.

November 5—Genesis 2:8-9, 15
What do these verses tell you about the Garden of Eden, where God put Adam and Eve?

November 6—Deuteronomy 4:15-19
Although we're supposed to respect the earth, what warning do these verses give?

November 7—Psalm 147:7-11
God takes care of His creation, but what He really enjoys is . . .

November 8—Isaiah 51:6
Dear God, even though the earth may be destroyed one day, thank You that . . .

November 9—Luke 21:25-28
Why can you feel hope even when natural disasters continue to happen all over the world?

November 10—Genesis 3:17-19

What do these verses tell you is a main cause of problems in the environment?

November 11—Isaiah 65:17-25

How do you feel about God's promises in these verses?

It's a Wrap!

Here are some fun ways to reuse wrapping paper you've taken off a gift:

 cover a book or journal

 make place mats for the dinner table

 if it's really pretty, put a piece of it in a frame and hang it up

 cut it to stationery size and write letters on the back

 make colorful paper airplanes or snowflakes

Extra! Next time you wrap a gift for a friend, use pages from a coloring book. You can either color the pages yourself or leave them for your friend to color. (You can tuck a little box of crayons into the ribbon or stick it onto the package with tape.)

Furry, Feathery Friends
Animal Acronyms

When you take a word and use each letter as the beginning of another word to form a title or phrase, that's called an acronym. For example, a well-known Christian acronym is:

FROG = fully rely on God

Here are a few more:

DOG = depend on God

BAT = believe and trust

OWL = obey with love

Now, try making up some of your own. (Warning: It's not as easy as it looks!)

Ferrets, Frogs, or Felines?

Here's what some girls in a recent survey said are their favorite animals:

Dogs . . . because they are pretty and nice most of the time and because you can cuddle with them and they are always happy to see you

Cats . . . because they are nice to cuddle up with

Horses . . . because they are beautiful and you can ride them

Giraffes . . . because of their long necks and spots

Frogs . . . because they can be cute

Dolphins . . . because they are really pretty, interesting, and very smart

Here are the animals they said make the best pets:

Dogs or cats . . . because they are easier to take care of than big animals

Dogs . . . because you can cuddle with them and always have a friend

Fish . . . because they are easy to look after and no one is allergic to them

Hamsters . . . because they are not that big of a responsibility and they're cute and fluffy

A Kooka-What?

You may think you know a lot about animals, but do you recognize these names? Look up each one in an encyclopedia or on the Internet and either draw a picture of it or write down some interesting facts about it. Then quiz your friends and see if they know these animals!

Kookaburra	Marmot	Wapiti	Emu	Agouti
Jerboa	Okapi	Pangolin	Civet	Ermine

Many people wonder whether or not animals have souls—especially people who have a pet that died. It's normal to become attached and close to your pets, especially dogs and cats, and to wish that you will see them again in heaven. The Bible doesn't say anything about pets being in heaven, but it clearly tells us that

God created humans in a very special way—breathing life into us and giving us souls. We're not just creatures that have evolved from another kind of animal . . . we're incredibly precious to God! But we must still respect and take care of the wonderful animals that God made for us to enjoy.

November 12—Proverbs 12:10
How does God want us to treat animals?

November 13—Job 12:7-10
What can you learn from the way nature and animals respect God?

November 14—Genesis 1:24-28
What kind of relationship did God make between humans and animals when He created them?

November 15—Luke 15:3-7
What comparison did Jesus make between a lost sheep and a sinner?

November 16—Psalm 50:10-11

Something these verses tell me about the way God sees
animals is . . .

November 17—Proverbs 6:6-8

Dear God, please help me to learn this lesson from ants:

November 18—Jeremiah 8:7

How does this verse make you feel about your knowledge of God?

Animal Quackers!

When you hear or see the words *baa, tweet tweet*, and *ribbit*, do
you think of sheep, birds, and frogs? If so, you probably live in
North America. Here's how people around the world express different animal sounds:

Hungary: *mek mek* (goat)
Greece: *tsiou tsiou* (bird)
Japan: *kero kero* (frog)
Italy: *ioh ioh* (donkey)
Sweden: *kuckeliku* (rooster)
France: *coin coin* (duck)

Section 7

THE MEDIA AND YOU

God designed your heart with just a single spot for number one. Are you letting the stuff you watch, read, and listen to influence who gets that spot?

Good "Ad"vice

Don't Get Reeled In

If you've ever gone fishing, you know that some bait at the end of a hook will attract a fish, and then . . . *whoosh!* . . . before the fish knows what's happening, it's reeled out of the water and tossed into a bucket!

Advertisers also use bait to get your attention, hoping you'll buy whatever they're selling. Take a look at what some of these companies do to convince you that you need their stuff:

* You couldn't actually eat most of the food you see in commercials because they're covered in "makeup" to make them look tasty. For example, white glue is often used instead of milk in cereal commercials (so the cereal doesn't get soggy), food coloring and Vaseline are sometimes brushed onto a hamburger to make it look juicy, and dishwashing liquid gets squirted into hot chocolate to make the bubbles last longer.

* Toy commercials often show accessories that aren't included with the toy when someone buys it. Also, the toy advertisers may make the toy look bigger than it really is, and they never show the boring part of putting the toy together before it can be played with.

Ads use celebrities or popular music to help you remember the products being sold. Advertisers hope that if you remember something you saw in a commercial, you will buy it the next time you see it.

 Most of all, advertisers tell you that if you don't buy their stuff, you won't be as cool as other people or you won't have as much fun. Don't believe it!

Hidden Messages

Did you know that the average person under the age of eighteen in the United States, Australia, and the United Kingdom sees about 30,000 commercials in one year?

The problem is, commercials don't just try to get you to buy things. Sometimes they have a bigger influence on how you think of yourself. You may start comparing yourself to the girls you see in ads and think that you need to be like them. If the models look really thin and wear sexy outfits, you may feel bad about your own body and looks. If the models seem rich and popular, you may think your life isn't good enough. These are not healthy messages!

Tip: Instead of thinking about things you may not have, do your best to feel thankful for everything you *do* have. You'll be much happier!

"Ad" Them Up!

This week, try to keep track of how many TV commercials, magazine advertisements, radio announcements, or billboards you are exposed to each day. How many of those ads made you want to buy something, go somewhere, or do something you normally wouldn't?

Day of the week	How many ads I saw	How the ads influenced me
Sunday		
Monday		
Tuesday		
Wednesday		
Thursday		
Friday		
Saturday		

You can't avoid commercials and advertisements—they're everywhere! Of course, not all advertising is bad: Sometimes you learn important information, and sometimes the ads have nothing to do with you and you can ignore them. But a lot of advertising encourages you to buy or participate in things that God may not want for you. Ask God to help you be more careful about how you are influenced by the messages around you.

November 19—Leviticus 10:10

Dear God, when I see advertisements, please give me wisdom to . . .

ignore them.

November 20—Deuteronomy 18:9

What does this verse tell you about being influenced by the messages you hear and see from the world around you?

November 21—Psalm 119:125-128

How can you make sure that you love God more than you love the stuff you see in commercials?

November 22—Hosea 14:9

Where can you find the wisdom that will keep you from being hooked by the influences around you?

November 23—2 Peter 1:3-4

How does God help you say no to things that aren't good for you?

November 24—1 Peter 4:1-5

What do these verses tell you about the difference between how a Christian should live and how the world tries to influence you?

....

....

November 25—Hebrews 5:11-14

Dear God, please help me become spiritually mature so that . . .

....

....

Let Jesus Influence You!

Try this: Whenever you find yourself wanting something in a commercial, think about something that God asks you to do in the Bible. Which message do you want to listen to? Instead of trying to become the person you're told to be in advertisements, try to be the kind of girl that you know *Jesus* wants you to be. You may even notice yourself becoming a positive influence on others!

Meaningful Music

Worship the Lord!

Use the chart below to solve this puzzle. Check your answer by reading Psalm 147:7.

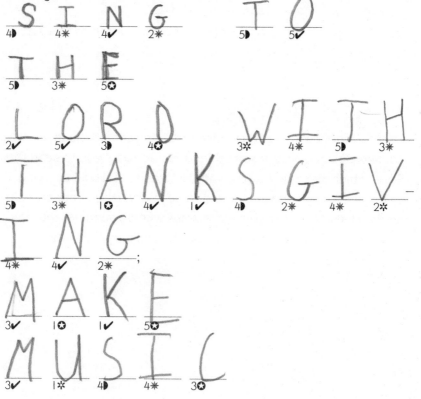

S I N G   T O
4● 4✳ 4✔ 2✳   5● 5✔

T H E
5● 3✳ 5✪

L O R D   W I T H
2✔ 5✔ 3● 4✪   3✴ 4✳ 5● 3✳

T H A N K S G I V-
5● 3✳ 1✪ 4✔ 1✔ 4● 2✳ 4✳ 2✴

I N G;
4✳ 4✔ 2✳

M A K E
3✔ 1✪ 1✔ 5✪

M U S I C
3✔ 1✴ 4● 4✳ 3✪

260

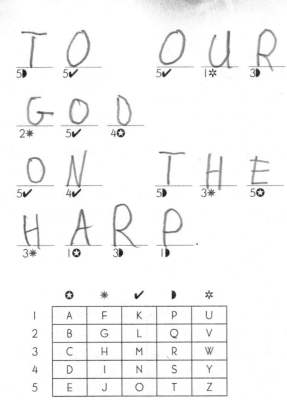

T O   O U R
5▸ 5✔   5✔ 1✻ 3▸

G O D
2✳ 5✔ 4✪

O N   T H E
5✔ 4✔   5▸ 3✳ 5✪

H A R P.
3✳ 1✪ 3▸ 1▸

	✪	✳	✔	▸	✻
1	A	F	K	P	U
2	B	G	L	Q	V
3	C	H	M	R	W
4	D	I	N	S	Y
5	E	J	O	T	Z

The Power of Music

How do you choose the music you listen to? Suggestions from your friends? Cute band members? Strong music? Good lyrics? You may not think it really matters what you listen to, but it does!

You can probably figure out that songs with bad language or words that promote things like sex, violence, drugs, suicide, and disobedience don't please God. Unfortunately, most of the music

SOLUTION: Sing to the LORD with thanksgiving; make music to our God on the harp.

261

out there is just like that. What makes this problem worse is that it's not just the words that are harmful to you. Doctors and scientists have discovered that music can affect your brain and heart! Certain types of music can speed up your heart rate, and others can cause depression or make sleeping difficult. Music has a big influence on your mood and attitude.

Pay close attention to what you listen to. If you sense that your music isn't helping you be your best as a Christian tween, start exploring other types of music. There's a lot of good music out there—especially Christian music!

Turn That Down!

Have your parents ever told you to turn your music down because you were playing it too loud? It's always important to obey your parents, of course, but listening to them on this subject will also do you a lot of good. Blasting your music can harm your relationships with people if you're bothering them . . . and it can also cause serious damage to your ears!

Sound volume is measured in decibels. If you hear noise louder than 85 decibels for a long time, you can harm your hearing. Noise above 140 decibels can cause damage right away. If your music is louder than a hair dryer, a vacuum cleaner, a noisy restaurant, or a ringing telephone . . . turn it down!

Here's a good rule to remember: Whenever you put music on, keep the volume at half the level (or less) of the possible volume on your player. The music will still sound great . . . and your ears will enjoy music for many more years to come!

Music is a gift from God! We read a lot about music and singing in the Bible, and many verses tell us to use music to worship and praise God. Sadly, a lot of the music out there does not honor God. In fact, some songs even contain evil messages. You need to be careful about what you allow into your mind. Make sure that the songs you hear and sing please God.

November 26—Psalm 92:1-4

Why is it good to praise the Lord?

It is good because you get to know Him better.

November 27—Psalm 95:1-6

What are some ways you can worship God?

Singing, praying, obeying.

November 28—Ephesians 5:19-20

What kind of attitude does God want you—and your music—to have?

A good attitude

November 29—1 John 2:15-17

I need to be careful about what kind of music I listen to because . . .

Some songs have an evil message and don't please God.

November 30—Ecclesiastes 7:4-5

How does the Bible warn about listening to "fools"? What does that tell you about how you should choose your music?

Says to listen to wise not fools. Choose music wisely.

December 1—1 Samuel 16:14-23

How do different types of music influence us?

how we think

December 2—Psalm 98

Dear God, I want to honor You with my music because . . .

I love you and want to honor you.

A Different Kind of Rock Concert

In Luke 19:37-40, Jesus told the Pharisees (religious leaders) that if His disciples weren't allowed to praise Him loudly in the streets, the rocks and stones would shout out loud!

That's a good reminder not to feel shy about telling others about the wonderful things God has done. One way you can do that is through the music you listen to and the songs you sing. There's a lot of noisy, confusing, and just plain bad music in the world today. Make sure *your* music brings glory and honor to Jesus. That shouldn't be the job of rocks and stones!

Whatcha Watchin'?

Tuned Out?

Watching television may not seem like such a terrible thing, especially if you feel that your favorite shows are not bad because they don't have much violence or swearing or sex. What you may not realize is that it isn't just what you watch that can harm you, it's *how much* you watch.

Here are just a few things that happen when you watch too much TV:

 You spend less time with your family, and your relationships with your parents and brothers and sisters get weaker. Studies show that Americans watch about four hours of television every day but spend less than one hour a week talking with their families!

 You spend less time reading and studying. You don't learn as quickly or do as well in school, and your creativity and imagination are damaged.

 You spend less time moving around and exercising, and you can become less healthy and possibly gain too much weight.

 You become more materialistic because you see thousands of commercials that influence you to want things.

 Your eyes hardly move as they try to catch everything happening on the screen. This can ruin your observation skills.

When you think about how television affects you, doesn't it make you want to spend your time better? In the space below, write down some things you can do this week instead of watching television. Here are some ideas to get you started:

- play a board game with your family
- do a puppet show
- write letters to friends or relatives
- do a jigsaw puzzle
- bake something
- go for a nature walk

*read
* play games
* play on computer
* have a nap

"I find television very educating. Every time somebody turns on the set, I go into the other room and read a book."
Groucho Marx (a famous comedian who died in 1977)

God Is Watching Too!

The movies and TV shows you watch have a great influence on your mind and heart. You may think you can handle hearing some swear words, watching violence, or seeing people do sexy things. Don't put too much confidence in yourself, though . . . we can't always control how those things influence our minds!

 266

God wants you to keep your mind pure and holy. Make the decision not to watch things that don't please and honor Him. Remember, whenever you turn on the TV, pop in a DVD, or go to the movies, He's right there with you!

The Bible doesn't say anything about television or movies—they obviously didn't exist at the time it was written! But the Bible still gives us a lot of good advice about what we allow into our minds and about how we spend our time. As you read these verses, ask God for wisdom in deciding what to watch. If watching TV has become a bad habit for you, ask Him to help you make better use of your time. You can do it! (By the way, there's a spot at the end of this week's devos for you to write down things you did instead of watching TV. Take a look!)

December 3—Matthew 12:35
What does this verse tell you about what you should store up inside your mind and heart?

What is good comes out good, what is evil comes out evil

December 4—2 Corinthians 7:1
To keep my soul pure, I need to make these changes to what I watch on TV and in movies:

change how many swears they say.

December 5—Matthew 6:22-23

Why should you be careful about what your eyes see?

December 6—2 Timothy 3:1-5

If these verses describe what you see on TV or in movies, what do you think God wants you to do?

December 7—Isaiah 26:9

How does the first part of this verse compare with how much time you spend thinking about God?

December 8—Psalm 39:5

It may be hard to imagine, but this verse says that life is short. How do you think you should spend your time?

December 9—Ephesians 5:15-16

Dear God, please help me use my time to . . .

Watch Yourself!

This week, every time you decide to do another activity instead of watching television, write down what you did. Then write how you felt afterward. At the end of the week, you may discover you had a lot more fun without television!

Sunday: made a bracelet.

Monday: played with sister

Tuesday: Tag's b-day read a book

Wednesday: read a book

Thursday: sang

Friday: went to school

Saturday: went 4 a walk

Food for Your Brain

What's on Your Book Menu?

These days you have thousands of books to choose from. The problem is, a lot of the literature you find in libraries and bookstores is like junk food for your brain . . . *and* heart! Many books teach confusing messages and lessons, and some go against what the Bible teaches and what God wants for you.

It's not always easy to know if a book is right for you. Ask your parents or another Christian adult to help you choose good books. There are a lot of good books out there that you may enjoy . . . and that are honoring to God. When you choose books to read, try to make sure they don't encourage things like bad behavior, sexual activity, violence, bad language, disrespect of God and the Bible, or witchcraft.

Here are some helpful questions to ask yourself:

 Would Jesus have chosen this book for me?

 Will this book help me develop my mind, heart, or character?

 Why do I really want to read this book—and is that a motive that would please God?

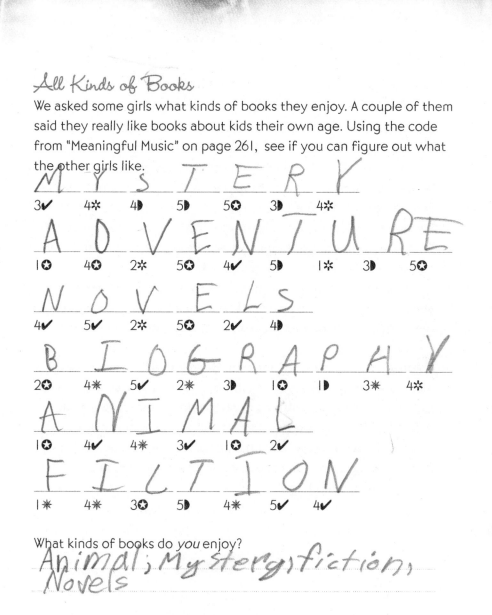

All Kinds of Books

We asked some girls what kinds of books they enjoy. A couple of them said they really like books about kids their own age. Using the code from "Meaningful Music" on page 261, see if you can figure out what the other girls like.

M Y S T E R Y
3✔ 4✽ 4◗ 5◗ 5✪ 3◗ 4✽

A D V E N T U R E
1✪ 4✪ 2✽ 5✪ 4✔ 5◗ 1✽ 3◗ 5✪

N O V E L S
4✔ 5✔ 2✽ 5✪ 2✔ 4◗

B I O G R A P H Y
2✪ 4✽ 5✔ 2✽ 3◗ 1✪ 1◗ 3✽ 4✽

A N I M A L
1✪ 4✔ 4✽ 3✔ 1✪ 2✔

F I C T I O N
1✽ 4✽ 3✪ 5◗ 4✽ 5✔ 4✔

What kinds of books do *you* enjoy?

Animal; Mystery; fiction; Novels

Magazine Mania

The girls we talked to said their favorite features in magazines are quizzes, posters, and animal pictures. What about you?

Magazines can teach you lots of interesting things about the world, people, science, or life. They sometimes give good advice or have fun activities, such as puzzles and quizzes. You need to be careful, though, because many teen magazines can also get your focus off of God and onto celebrities, fashion, beauty, and gossip. Some magazines make things that are wrong seem cool, and they can start influencing the way you think.

Next time you pick up a magazine—or read one online—think about what you're about to feed your mind. You may decide to read a good book or your Bible instead. Hey, what a great idea!

Some of you may enjoy reading. You might like comic books, magazines, thick novels, short stories, or poetry. But even if reading isn't your favorite activity, it's good to take time each day to do it. Reading helps you learn and it develops your brain cells. But reading the wrong stuff can be harmful for you! As you read your Bible this week, ask God to help you know what to read and what books or magazines to get rid of.

December 10—Ecclesiastes 12:9-12

What do these verses tell you about being careful with what you read?

December 11—Acts 8:26-31, 35

What can you do when you're reading something that you don't understand?

December 12—1 Timothy 4:7

Dear God, instead of my wasting time reading things that will confuse my mind, please help me to . . .

read things that make me closer to you.

December 13—Psalm 139:15-17

How is your relationship with God different from your relationship with human authors?

December 14—Romans 8:5-8

Why is it important to be careful about what fills your mind?

December 15—Hebrews 3:1

If my thoughts are supposed to be focused on Jesus, then the reading material I choose should . . .

December 16—John 21:25

How does this verse make you feel about how much time you spend reading about Jesus?

TIP #1: Ask your church librarian, youth group leader, or Sunday school teacher to suggest some good books for you to read.

TIP #2: Don't spend too much time reading books and magazines that are just fun and that don't teach you anything useful or don't help you grow as a Christian. Make time to read your Bible, too!

Online . . . or Out of Line?

It's a Big World Out There!

It's probably hard for you to imagine a world without the Internet, e-mail, blogs, cell phones, iPods, and instant messaging. But just five or ten years before you were born, these were unfamiliar things to most people. Technology has been advancing so fast it's hard to keep up with all the new stuff you can do or buy!

E-mail, text messaging, and webcams can help you feel close and connected with friends or relatives—whether they live down the street or halfway around the world. That's one of the good things that technology has done for us. Unfortunately, technology has also made it easier to meet *unfriendly* people, or to see things you shouldn't.

This week, ask God to help you understand the dangers of the Internet and to make smart choices when you go online. And as we discussed about TV and movies, you may want to think about how much time you spend in front of the computer screen, too.

Not Just Fun and Games!

So . . . how often are you on the Internet? Are there guidelines in your house about how long you can spend online and what sites you can go on? What do you usually use the Internet for? Research? Games? Keeping up with friends?

You need to be aware that along with the good parts of the Internet, there are also potential dangers:

 Having a stranger start chatting with you. Sometimes these are adults pretending to be people your age. They may later try to get you to meet them. *Never* chat with people if you're not completely sure who they are. Ask one of your parents to check who it is.

 Giving away too much information. Again, don't talk to strangers online . . . and never share personal information online (in chat rooms, on your blog or Web page, or anywhere else!). That includes your address, phone number, photos of your house, information about your parents' jobs, or what school you go to. Also, don't reply to e-mails from strangers. A message from you can give them information you didn't mean for them to have.

 Receiving rude or cruel messages or pictures through e-mail, text messages, or online posts. This is called cyber-bullying.

 Finding pornography. Even an innocent search on the Internet can bring up pictures or Web sites with sexual content. You may feel grossed out at first, but it can be tempting to keep looking. Don't start a habit that can be very hard to break! If you find yourself going back to this type of material, ask your parents to set up a good filter on your computer. Talk to someone you trust, and come up with

 275

a plan of action for when you feel tempted. (For example, walk away from the computer, do something else you enjoy, and pray!)

 Downloading illegal material. The law is very strict about copying music, movies, and other types of material without permission. Besides the fact that you're stealing someone else's stuff, you can get caught. Ask a parent to help you check if you're allowed to download something before you do.

You can find many versions of the Bible on the Internet . . . but you won't find anything about the Internet in the Bible! So how can you know what God thinks about your time online? As with other subjects that the Bible doesn't really mention, it always helps to understand God's character and how He expects you to live your life.

December 17—1 Timothy 6:11

You may find a lot of harmful but tempting things on the Internet. How should you respond when that happens?

December 18—Ephesians 2:10

This verse says God created you to do good works. How does that make you feel about the time you spend and the things you do online?

December 19—Galatians 5:16

The best way for me to keep from giving in to temptation is to . . .

December 20—John 3:20-21

Do you look at Web sites or do things online that you keep a secret from your parents? What do these verses tell you about that?

December 21—Amos 5:14

Dear God, please help me to . . .

December 22—Psalm 46:1

How can this verse help you when you feel confused or troubled about online situations?

December 23—Proverbs 2:1-5, 9-11

Where can you find the wisdom you need when you're online?

Write It Down!

In the space below, write down the guidelines you have at home about using the Internet. If you're not sure, have a chat with your parents! Is there anything you need to add or change?

No Other Gods

You Need Role Models . . . Not Idols!

There's *American Idol, Canadian Idol, Australian Idol,* and *Pop Idol* (in the United Kingdom). Notice anything similar about the titles of these shows, in which people compete to become the next great star? Do you know what an idol actually is?

Anything (or anyone) that someone worships and gives more importance to than God is an idol. In the Ten Commandments, God clearly warned against having idols.

It's natural to admire people and to want the admiration of others, but watch that no one comes before God in your life. Instead, look for "real" people—people you actually know—whose example and good character you can learn from. We all need role models, but not idols!

Who Do You Look Up To?

Laurie admires a girl who works at the Society for the Prevention of Cruelty to Animals. "I like her job, and one day I would like to have one like hers. She teaches people about how to take care of animals."

Courtney looks up to her mom because "she loves me and takes care of me, and she's a good influence on me. She does a lot of volunteering." She also admires her cousin Amanda because "she's really cool and nice."

Kristen says her friends Sam and Chantal are her role models. "They are mature, nice, pretty, and a good example for me, and I should live up to them."

Emma thinks of her mom as a role model because "she takes good care of us. I want to follow God just like she does." She also admires Mia Hamm, a professional soccer player.

This week, take time to thank your role models for their positive influence in your life. Give them hugs, send thank-you notes, or call them!

"Follow My Example"

In 1 Corinthians 11:1, the apostle Paul said, "Follow my example, as I follow the example of Christ." Paul wasn't saying that he was a super-Christian, but he could encourage others to follow his example because he was following Jesus. He wasn't trusting his own wisdom or strength, as some people do.

Can your friends follow you? Where would they end up? If you're following Jesus, God can use you as a good role model for others . . . no matter how old or young you are!

Christian singer Ginny Owens says, "I don't get up in the morning and think I'm a role model, but I know that preteens always look up to people older than them, so I want to make sure the things I do and say set a good example. . . . Preteens are also called to be role models: for first- and second-graders, for example."

Ask God to prepare you to be someone's role model. You never know what kind of positive influence you may have on someone's life!

No one, no matter how smart or talented or rich or even nice that person seems, deserves your worship. God, your Designer, belongs in the number one spot in your life. This week, pray and ask God to show you if there are things that you give a higher priority to than Him. It's our last week of devotions . . . but the adventure isn't over! Continue celebrating and using your designer genes by living for God every day!

December 24—Matthew 4:8-10
What can you learn from Jesus' example in these verses?

December 25—Psalm 40:4-5
These verses teach me that . . .

December 26—Exodus 20:3-4
What does the Bible say about having idols?

December 27—Psalm 115:2-8

How are idols different from our living God?

December 28—Habakkuk 2:18-20

Why are human-made idols worthless?

December 29—Ezekiel 14:2-6

If you have idols in your heart, what should you do?

December 30—Psalm 96:1-6

Dear God, I give You first place in my life because . . .

Today's Idols

In some parts of the world you may find people who still bow down to and worship statues or other objects, just like many men and women in the Old Testament did. But those aren't the only gods people have. Take a look at the society you live in and see

if you can identify idols that people have today. Some examples include money, clothes, and popularity. What else do you think people worship?

Before You Go . . .

Hello friend,

I hope you enjoyed reading *Designer Genes* as much as I enjoyed writing it! Maybe you and I have never met each other, but I kind of feel like we've become friends this past year. I wish we could go get ice cream together and you could tell me all about what you've done and discovered in the last twelve months!

Some of the devos we did were fun, and some were serious. We used our imaginations, we laughed, we tried to be better friends and daughters and sisters, we talked to God, we thought about our goals and priorities, we took better care of ourselves, we learned a lot of interesting things, and we explored the most amazing book—the Bible!

My prayer is that each devo helped you to learn more about your Designer . . . and yourself! I hope *Designer Genes* answered some of your questions and gave you confidence that you are God's awesome and precious work of art. Most of all, I hope that if you didn't know Jesus when you started reading this book, you do now.

Keep *Designer Genes* in a special place, and go through it sometimes to remind yourself about things you learned and promises you made. You may be amazed to see how much you've grown and matured since you first started reading this book!

If there's anything you want to tell me about *Designer Genes*, or if you have some questions, you can contact me on the Web site www.designergenesdevo.wordpress.com!

Ann-Margret Housepian

One Last Thing . . .

Before you put this book away, let's dig in to the Bible one more time and read 1 Peter 2:2-3. Write down how you think you've grown spiritually in the past year and what your goals are for the year ahead.

_____

_____

_____

_____

_____

_____

_____

_____

P.S. Your designer genes look really good! I'm sure a lot of people will notice what a great girl you're becoming . . . from the inside out! Just remember to stay close to God, your great Designer. He loves you!

Scripture Index

Check out these other One Year Devos:

The One Year Devos for Teens

The One Year Devos for Teens 2

The One Year Devos for Sports Fans

Get your own copy today!

CP018